HOW I LOST
5 POUNDS IN
6 YEARS

HOW I LOST 5 POUNDS IN 6 YEARS

An Autobiography

Tom Arnold

St. Martin's Press ✼ *New York*

www.stmartins.com

ISBN 0-312-29134-5

First Edition: November 2002

10 9 8 7 6 5 4 3 2 1

To Shelby, my D.C.T.
Thank you for now, forever. I love you.

Acknowledgments

Dad—my hero in so many ways.

Dottie, Dort, Tom, and D.B.—I'm doing good, but I miss you guys every day.

Mom—I think I'm finally ready to talk.

Ruth—thanks for making Dad a home and making him very happy.

Chris—thanks for the laughs, the weirdness, and being the family middleman.

Mark—nice guy, good dad, be careful.

Marla—easy does it, try not to get bitter.

Lori—but for the grace of God . . .

Johnny—good husband and dad, *and* Jesus loves him!

Scott—from what I hear, you're on your way.

Josh—be careful in whose footsteps you follow.

Mo—a guy could not have a better friend.

Charity—for letting Mo hang.

Mike Sporer—thanks for the friendship and free food.

Brownie and Cox—we gotta do better at staying in touch.

The Tisches—thank you for your unwavering friendship. How else could a guy like me summer in the Hamptons (or Aspen)?

Acknowledgments

The Davis Family and Kenny—the parties, the gifts, the gossip, the drama. Your friendship has improved my life in so many ways.

Jack and Shirley Fry—you were nice to me before I could afford to pay people to be nice to me.

David Carr—the promises do come true, buddy (even if you are working for the tightass *New York Times*).

Ann Marie—thank you for your kindness (and your daughter). *Nobody* makes a better tuna casserole.

Melissa—Shelby could not have a better sister (please don't cry).

Mike Roos—you are a good father and a class act (although I'm being punished for any small mistakes you did make).

My "Team": Daniel Rappaport, Lee Stollman, Staci Wolfe, Dave Feldman, and Mel Berger—did any of you even read this book?

St. Martin's Press, Sally Richardson, Jennifer Weis, and Joanna Jacobs—thanks for the encouragement, the few but perfect notes, and for letting me do it.

John Murphy—thanks in advance. I just know you're going to be a big help.

Feinstein and Berson—for getting me back to one.

Marnie, Brian, and Jonathan—I want what you have.

Budd Friedman—thanks for the stage.

Kathleen Manley and Mrs. Coffin—World's Best Baby-Sitters.

Betty Ford—for introducing me to my disease.

Maria Shriver—thanks for the great advice, but nobody would listen!

Arnold—everybody's hero.

Jim Cameron—thank you. Now where the hell are you?

Joel Silver—thanks for the jobs. I know, I know, next time I'll get paid.

Andrzej Bartkowiak—you always make it fun.

Ed and Pam McMahon—friends with class.

Stephen, Pam, and Brad—to the future.

Acknowledgments

David Letterman—thanks for letting me be funny.

Jay Leno—thanks for doing so much and laughing at my pain.

Bob Hope—thanks for making Dad laugh, so damn hard.

Johnny Carson—for doing it right.

Bill Maher—face the real danger, buddy, get married!

Richard Pryor—thank you for your brilliance and sorry I stepped on your foot.

Howard Stern—you get me in so much trouble.

Conan O'Brien—try and relax, buddy! Thanks for your weirdness.

Craig Kilborn—funniest jock ever.

Lorne Michaels—thank you. Now if I could just get back on the show. . . .

Stan Winston—for showing me that some things are worth fighting for.

Brandon—I'm proud of you.

Hilary—you've really grown, stay in touch.

Chris Farley—miss you, buddy.

Johnny and Kevin Farley—keep up the good work.

Fox Sports—thanks, but what the hell were you thinking?

Michael Rosenbaum—"I know, buddy, it's huge."

Kat—I know you hated every second of it, but thanks for keeping me on track.

David Wells—thanks for the friendship and the tickets.

Gina Meyer—thank you but I bet it's embarrassing to tell people you are my trainer.

Kathie Lee—one nice gal.

The multitalented Don Roos—I wish I was you (except for the gay part).

The Tuesday Night Gang—I always feel better when it's over.

Dr. Drew—I know, I'm sick.

Stephen Shapiro—nothing like a hot young wife, eh, buddy. Hurry up and get famous so we can roast you!

Marty Singer—nobody fucks with Marty Singer.

Acknowledgments

Laura Kahwaji—thanks for scrambling.

Val and Susie—for staying in touch.

Roseanne—for the many good times, the other stuff ain't that important.

Jenny, Jess, Jake, and Brandy—at least we have some good stories.

Tom Amross—Kate's Kitchen just ain't the same.

Jan, Heidi, Denise, and Kim—thank you for your time and for wanting me to be my best. I wish you all well.

Bob and Kay—my crazy-ass godparents.

Zach and May—my perfect godchildren.

Doug Maynard, J. C. Burns, Herm Kurtz, Doug Nelson, and Uncle Bill Cooper—all gone too damn soon.

The People of Iowa, especially Ottumwa—thank you for the support and for never changing.

Indian Hills Community College and the University of Iowa— for changing my life.

The Fans (like I actually have them!)—for all the encouragement.

The guys and gals back in the day at Hormel and meatpackers everywhere!

Scott Hansen—thanks for the work.

Mrs. Thompson—my ninth-grade drama teacher, who gave me encouragement and good advice, like what to do if you get an erection during the makeout scene from *Anne of a Thousand Days* (exit stage left).

Aunt Linda—always.

Sid Youngers, Joel Madison, Joel Hodgson, Alex Cole, Mike Gandolfi, Don Foster, Dave Raether, Wild Bill Bauer, Tom Frykman, Joe Keys, Joe Minjares, and all the other Minneapolis Comedy All-Stars.

Charlie Dickey (lawn work), Kevin O'Brien (McDonald's), Chris Buff (Kinney's Shoes), Les Moonves (CBS, Warner Bros.), Bob Iger (ABC)—damn fine bosses all.

Snuffy—I know you're there if I need you.

Shaq—father, author, actor, rapper, baller, neighbor. If you move, I'm going with you.

Constance Schwartz—welcome to L.A., baby!

Dawn Steel—"Tom, please don't become an asshole." Okay.

Chris Kirkpatrick—my favorite boy-band boy.

Dr. Paul—am I cured now?

Bill Bixby—for the enthusiasm.

Kelly Stone—thanks for looking out for the little guys.

Geoff and Russ Courtnall—let's *not* invest in any new companies, but thanks for finding Shelby.

The Shriver family—for changing the way we look at people.

Prince—for letting me sing at the Hollywood Bowl (sorry I forgot the frickin' words).

The kids and everyone involved with the San Diego Center for Children.

Hill, Dolgen, Greenberg, Mayer, E.W., Shanks, Lisa G., Lee Ann, Farr, Salley, Kruk, Rose, Irvin, the producer's crew, the writers, and the girls of B.D.S.S.P.—I couldn't work with a better team.

Pat O'Brien—I'm still really sorry about your arm.

Stedman Graham—I still have to look at my license once in a while.

Rabbi Freehling—tough times, loving advice.

Rabbi Borowitz—for helping Brandon and so many others.

To the directors who put up with me: Cameron, Bartkowiak, Stephen Frears, Herbert Ross, Chris Columbus, Jay Roach, Paul Schrader, Steve Buscemi, John Landis, Arthur Hiller, Peter Segal, John Whitesall, John Pasquin, Steve Minor, Bryan Spicer, Andy Weyman, Mark Medoff, Michael Lessac, Will McKensie, Todd Phillips, Steve Chase, Jeff Margolis, Phillip Charles McKensie, Amanda Bearse, Tobe Hooper, Bill Bixby, and many more. . . .

And to some of the fine actors I got to work with: Arnold, Jamie Lee Curtis, Dustin, Roseanne, John Goodman, Laurie Metcalf, Estelle Parsons, Ben Stiller, Jerry Stiller, Jim Carrey, Robin

Acknowledgments

Williams, Hugh Grant, Joan Cusack, Julianne Moore, Don Knotts, Allison La Placa, Paul Feig, Carol Kane, Stephen Rea, Michael Boatman, Chris Farley, Adam Sandler, Sandra Bernhard, Jessica Lundy, Rachael Leigh Cook, DMX, Jet Li, Anthony Anderson, Drag-On, Rick Moranis, Janeane Garofalo, Charlton Heston, Christopher Walken, Shaquille O'Neal, Jeff Goldblum, Liam Waite, Ashley Johnson, Mike Myers, Tim Curry, David Alan Grier, Henry Cho, Bruce Campbell, Dennis Quaid, Danton Stone, Kathleen Turner, Park Overall, Martin Mull, Fred Willard, Dan Ackroyd, Bill Paxton, Steven Seagal, Lolita Davidovich, Breckin Meyer, Will Farrell, David Spade, Paul Mazursky, Jon Tenney, Red Buttons, Jon Lovitz, Andy Dick, Robert Wuhl, Téa Leoni, Kirstie Alley, Michael Rosenbaum, Ed McMahon, Sara Gilbert, Sarah Chalke, Michael Fishman, Lecy Goranson, Andy Lawrence, Joey Lawrence, Matthew Lawrence, Christopher McDonald, Bob Odenkirk, Gina Gershon, Jean Smart, Shannon Tweed, Mary McDonald, Simon Rex, Gabrielle Union, John Ritter, Debra Messing, Dave Foley, Lisa Withoit, Dennis Boutsikaris, John Farley, Kevin Farley, Chris Issak, Bridget Fonda, Skeet Ulrich, George Wendt, Rob Schneider, Molly Shannon, Eddie Furlong, Cheri Oteri, Jayne Meadows, Eddie Griffin, Steve Allen, Tracy Morgan, William Forsythe, Kenneth Marks, Hill Harper, Amy Smart, Malcolm-Jamal Warner, Peter Facinelli, David Rasche, Amy Irving, Jay Fergeson, Colleen Camp, Shelly Winters, Ken Olin, Conchatta Ferrell, Patricia Wettig, Eliza Dushku, Danny Trejo, Mika Boorem, Kathie Lee Gifford, Mekhi Pfeiffer, Steve Buscemi, Rhea Pearlman, Willem Dafoe, Rod Steiger, Tiffani Thiessen, Hillary Danner, Sally Kirkland, Phil Hartman, David Paymer, Danielle Harris, Alex McKenna, Bug Hall, Ernest Borgnine, Dean Stockwell, Illeana Douglas, Shawnee Smith, French Stewart, Clarence Williams III, Ed Lauter, Ricky Jay, Brian Haley, Jeri Ryan, Jason Momoa, Harry Hamlin, Eddie Albert, Jeanetta Arnette, Ann Cusack, Thomas Ian Nicholas, Majandra Delfino, Julie Benz, Lisa Zane, Johnny Galecki, John Carpenter,

Acknowledgments

Tobe Hooper, Dave Foley, Dave Cronenberg, Atom Egoyan, Robert Wise, Frankie Faison, Jenny McCarthy, Costa-Gavras, Matt Keeslar, Mark Metcalf, Obba Babatunde, Julianne Phillips, Larry Miller, Jeffrey Tambor, Peter Jason, Jason Alexander . . . I know I'll think of more later.

Chloe, Charlie, and Cooper—we'll never have nice furniture, but I still love ya.

Thank you for doing me the honor of reading even one word of this book.

Introduction

This is a good time to be a Tom. But I wish this were a book by Tom Cruise. I'd like to know what makes him tick. But he probably wouldn't tell us. Doesn't have to; he's too smart and too successful. Real movie stars have an air of mystery. It's probably best that we don't find out the real truth about Tom, that he's just like us only a lot more talented and a hell of a lot better-looking. Yet I bet he's a little insecure. Otherwise, he probably wouldn't feel the need to make millions of strangers love him. Still, there's no denying that he's a handsome man. But I like Tom Cruise anyway, because when he laughs, he laughs hard. You've seen it; his nose wrinkles up and his teeth stick out. Throw a pair of black-framed glasses on him and you've got the star of *Revenge of the Nerds V*. I like a man that laughs hard.

Then there's Tom Hanks, the father of show business—no, the country, the world really. Space, too. No sarcasm intended to Mr. Oscar, the man is solid gold. Great movies, great wife, family, and only the finest friends, and yet Tom looks like he's getting tired, even a little crabby. I'll bet he longs for the simple *Bosom Buddies* days, when everything he did, every move he made, didn't have to be wonderful or at least perfect. Tom Hanks won't be writing any books for us unless it's something historical and important, with all the proceeds going to the kind of charity that makes grown men weep. Personally, I'd just be happy to see the man laugh more and harder.

After Tom Selleck, Tom Brokaw, and Tom Clancy, I may be the next most famous Tom in America, which is incredible, because I haven't really done anything incredible. Unless you consider the fact that the only advice my dad ever gave me was, "Tom, you can do anything you want in life, as long as you work at the meatpacking plant." He was right, you know. If I'd never worked at the meatpacking plant, I'd never have been able to appreciate my second career as a well-known semisuccessful actor/comedian/writer whose personal life has defied the old adage "There's no such thing as bad press." How can I possibly feel like a failure after spending three years covered in bloody pig debris? After all, I saw on TV that a man actually spent $45,000 for plastic surgery to look like me. Not to *not* look like me, but to look like me. Crazy, huh? Of all the Toms, he picks me. He probably requested a Cruise or a Hanks face and the doctor was like (Scottish accent), "Come on; I'm a surgeon, not a magician," and the guy's like, "What about Tom Arnold?" And Doctor said, "I can do that in my garage this weekend with a trowel and some spackle, but there's no going back." Sad thing is, that guy has probably gotten more work as me than I have as me these last few years. Originally, I wanted to call this book something fantastic like *T.A., The Great American Hero* or *T.A., Hollywood Superstar*, but the legal department said I would surely get sued for false advertising. So after carefully reviewing my life in pictures I went with what I had done. I had lost five pounds in six years. Not a great title for a self-help book, but that's okay because I am the one who needs the help. Something is missing from my life. Something I need. Something I cannot do without: a child. . . . You know, come to think of it, Tom Petty's pretty famous, too. And Tom Watson, Tom Berenger, Tom Jones, Tom Snyder, Tommy Tune, and Tom and Jerry, aw hell. . . .

Some guys have a nice childhood, grow up, go to school, start their career, marry their high school sweetheart, have a family, and live happily ever after. And some guys do things the hard way. My name is Tom Arnold. I am energetic, hygienic, and I can eat more food at one sitting than anybody I've ever met. Not bragging, just a fact. What more could you possibly need to know?

But I am writing this book for my child. Boy, girl, whatever. Doesn't matter, I just really want to be your dad. We haven't met you yet, but it's not for lack of trying. I've dreamed about you since I was a skinny eighteen-year-old longhair boning hams at the Hormel meatpacking plant back in Iowa. We would've been together by now, but I thought it would be best for both of us if I met your mother first. It's been a long twenty-five-year search, but I promise it will be worth the wait and you'll love her as much as I will. Let me tell you about her. Oh, she's kind, compassionate, affectionate, and patient and I may not deserve that, but you do, because you're a great kid. Most parents say their kids are great (mine didn't, but that generation "didn't believe in bullshit," according to my dad). But everybody *knows* how great you are. I'd like to take credit for this, but you will get it from your mom and that's why we have to be patient a little while longer. Patience is a virtue that I am still discovering.

Several good women have walked through my life (run actually), but they were not the ones for us. And God, with his infinite wisdom, has blessed me with a low sperm count just to keep me in line. Not to worry, though. I took the hamster test to see if I could reproduce. This is where they take the egg of a hamster and one of my sperm (don't worry; I've got dozens) and put them together. If my sperm can fertilize the hamster egg, the doctor gives me the all clear to move on to human women. I didn't sleep a wink the night of the test, but in the morning I got the most important call of my life: "Good news, Tom. The hamster is pregnant; let's move on to Step Two."

"Hold on, Doc, not so fast," I said. "Let's see how this hamster thing plays out." I was just thrilled to know that in a few months there would be a little Tomster running around. . . . Besides I had no human women or their eggs.

But I've been looking. Looking for a woman we will love and respect. Women eat that up. You'll be happy to know she and I will be best friends. Yes, I will demote all those I have known in my lifetime one big notch. The three of us will be a great team. She will be our barometer for what is good in the world. Some call this codependence. I call it true love. If you and I disagree she'll always take your side, which is OK, because I'm usually wrong and I promptly admit it. Besides, who am I kidding? I'll always take your side, too. And I will make sacrifices. Like, for instance, I guess having a kid is a supergood excuse for women to be too tired for sex. But I got that all worked out (see my chapter on masturbation). You'll feel safe with your mom and me. When I tell you everything is going to be all right, you believe it. You'll never go hungry. Although I wouldn't leave anything important for you in the fridge overnight, I can't be trusted. Mom will want us to be the best people we can be. She'll push us and we'll want to be perfect for her. She'll say things like, "You really shouldn't travel with a beautiful female assistant" (to me), "Don't play in the street" (to you), and "Keep your hands out of your pants" (to both of us). But she will unconditionally love us just the way we are. OK, that's a lot for me to ask, but it is my dream.

I've got a lead on a very good woman right now. She has all those great qualities *and* she's beautiful. I love her. She loves me, too, but she doesn't like saying it because it "encourages" me. Now, normally I'd think that she was out of my league. Even throwing my hat in the ring with a goddess of this magnitude

4

would be futile. And, sure, with the laws of nature being what they are, her lack of physical flaws technically makes her a different species from myself. But I've still got a little cash and I am famous and that's gotta take off ten years and twenty pounds. The sooner she gets old and fat, the better for my self-confidence. I've been known to be the jealous type. Read on; you'll understand. Besides, I've got to think of you, and once you see my family tree you'll understand the importance of adding some perfection to the stew of hair loss, bad dental design, alcoholism, and criminal hijinks boiling in the Arnold gene pot.

I think you'll be proud of the way I'm handling this delicate situation with this woman. After only five months I tricked her into living with me. I lured her in with a puppy. One of those nasty little fluffy white girlie dogs, which she just loves. She rubs *his* belly all the time, and when *he* gets "excited" she thinks it's funny. I wish somebody would rub my belly. Charlie, the dog, does lick me a lot. But she says he's just addicted to nicotine and sweat. Three months later, except for my occasional irrational but brief outbursts, I've given up being crabby (it reminded her of her dad). Now we've got two sissy mutts, Charlie and Chloe (Perfumes of the Seventies for $100, Alex Trebek), and her mom stops by and cooks for me (Mom's a member of the clean plate club, too—excellent grandma material). I finally got our gorgeous wife/mom finalist to throw away her spray-painted "art" and unpack most of her boxes. But this is the kicker: She gave away a table yesterday because there was no room in "our" house for it! *Our house.* I love it. This is so exciting! But I'll probably blow it, so I've got to try to remain calm. I know what you're thinking: "Dad, wouldn't it be enough to just be in a good relationship with one special person?" Not for me, not for most guys. When Tom Cruise said, "You complete me," to Renee Zellweger in *Jerry Maguire* he already knew that he was getting a kid in the bargain. Even Forrest Gump had a son.

Just a few years ago I seriously considered giving up on

women altogether (my accountant's and therapist's recommen-
dations) and traveling to China by myself to find you in one of
those orphanages I've read so much about. I can already see the
heartwarming story on *Entertainment Tonight*. Things are good
now at home, but I don't want to jump the gun. I've done that
a couple of times. Fortunately, you were not involved. Just a lot
of money, hurt feelings, and bad press. I promise you that I've
learned a lot from my mistakes and that I'm not going to follow
in my poor crazy mother's footsteps. She didn't like to "encourage" me, either. She never felt comfortable with the old "I love
you, son." But she did pinch me a lot, so I got what I needed. I
know she cared because once when I was six I ripped the crotch
out of my pants on the last day of my life that I didn't wear
underwear and she delicately warned me in front of all of her
pals at the Elks lodge that I was "about to lose a nut." Mom was
a hopeless romantic. She always told me, "No bastard is going
to buy the cow if he can get the milk for free." She was married
seven times in our small town before she was thirty-five. Needless to say, I got teased a lot. Let's hope you never have to hear,
"Your mom's a hose bag," from the other third graders.

I don't really remember much about my parents' divorce. One
day my mom was there and the next day she wasn't. I guess I
didn't feel so bad because I knew she wanted to leave. Her boyfriend wanted her to leave, too. And if there's one thing I've
learned, my child, it's that you can't make a woman stay if she
really wants to go. Not legally, anyway. So I dealt with it like a
good four-year-old should. But my little brother wasn't so mature. Scotty Potty (I guess I wasn't so mature, either) wet the
bed for ten years. I had two loving grandmothers and a father
who gave me everything he had (receding hairline, back acne,
and a devastating overbite). I guess I was lucky, but not as lucky
as you. You're getting me at my best.

Although I'm the oldest, smartest, and best-looking of the
seven Arnold children, I'm the only one who hasn't had the priv-

ilege of raising a child. Even my gay brother, Chris, was a foster parent. His son was released from state prison this year, after serving six years of an eighteen-month sentence. I guess he liked it there. He was busted for driving the getaway van during an ill-fated gas station heist to get some cash for pot and Iron Maiden tickets. I did help look after another nephew for ten years while his racketeering drug kingpin parents were away at the federal penitentiary. I also was a stepparent, but when their mom said good-bye (actually, she didn't say it—her lawyers and the *National Enquirer* did) they were instantly out of my life. All I have to show for almost five years of my time and energy are a few family photos, a wood thing they carved me at Fat Camp, and the memories of an occasional hug or an "I love you, Tom" when we said our good nights. Was it worth it? Hell, no. . . . OK, I'm lying. It was the best thing that ever happened to me. Until now.

Some friends have even asked me to be a godparent to their children. These are intelligent people. Why would they grace me with such an honor and responsibility? Is it because they feel sorry for me? Probably. Because they think they'll outlive me? Certainly. My therapist says it's also because they love and trust me and they believe that I am qualified for parenthood. Well then, so do I.

First of all, I've been sober for over twelve years. This is undeniably the best thing I ever did for us (but maybe not the best thing for the book, since everybody knows that all the best writers are drunks). I will (with the grace of God) never have to apologize to you for the kind of bad behavior that flows out of the practicing alcoholic/drug addict (bed-wetting, gunplay). But beware that as my child you will have to be extra careful. When I was young, I swore I'd never drink (although I didn't make any promises about crack). So I'm going to be watching out for you. No matter what happens, I've probably been there myself and can help. I *will* help (whether you ask for it or not). I'll be there night and day. So let's not go there—OK? That way I'll never have to whip out the "Tom's Tough Love." I'll do it if I have to, because I'm a pro, but I've got a feeling it's a lot easier to administer to other people's kids than my own. So instead, Mom and I will heap tons of love on you and build your self-esteem from day one. Fortunately, I haven't set the bar too high, so you won't have to live in my considerable shadow. If all that doesn't work and you get out of line, I swear to God I'll lock you in your room until you're sixty-five, and I am not kidding. Remember, I am famous. Your laws do not apply to me.

Second, I'm good dad material because I love myself. OK, *love* might be a strong word, but usually I do really, really like myself. OK, that's a lie, too. Sometimes I don't. Like when I think too much or I accidentally look in the mirror. But you *have* to love yourself. I know this is a lot to ask, especially as you get older, but I will teach you. When the chips are down—and if you're anything like your old man, a compulsive overeating, balding, twice-divorced fat guy, the chips get down a lot—you've got to pull yourself up and carry on like I always do. You know how your mom worries. You have to find that self-love that is deep down inside. Liposuction, liquid diets, hair transplants, and 12-Step meetings, you say? I know from experience sometimes that just isn't enough. That's when I surrender to a power greater than myself. I pull out a picture of little Tommy Arnold, age four. I look at that kid and a kind of magic happens. I get a warm feeling because he's so damn cute and sweet. Look at those big brown eyes. Darn it, I love that kid! And if I love him I guess I have to love the big old Tom, too! By God, I'm going to be all right! At least until the next time life deals me a crushing blow or my woman tells me no. . . .

I guess the final and best argument for me being your dad is that I'm fun. I'm working three jobs right now, but they are "show business" jobs, so I've usually got a lot of time on my hands, and I like to play. I promise to play with you for as long as you'll let me. My dad liked to play, too, but once he remarried, playtime was over. I had to learn how to play by myself. This is an art I have perfected that helps me to this day, but don't worry, because I will *always* play with you. And you will never have to humiliate yourself on some TV reality game show, because I will give you $1 million. That's right, $1 million. Mom, too, but I'm sure she'll know that going in. The person I was at eighteen, twenty-five, or even thirty-five is not the person I am today. It may have taken me all these years to grow into the kind of man who deserves a family like ours.

Now I'm going to tell you about my years of "growth." Partly to brag, because I suppose I'd love it if you thought I was cool. Unfortunately, I'm not cool. Never was. I wish I were. I tried being cool for a few years, but I know enough cool people now to know that I ain't cool. You know what dashing is? I'm the complete opposite of that. But maybe you'll think I'm kinda cool, at least until you're five or six. I don't expect it and I know I'm not going to get it from the wife, but if it happens for us that would be great. No pressure, though. I'm not even going to bring up being your hero. That's way too much to ask. Did I mention that I've done thirty-five movies? I guess I thought that I'd tell you about my life so that maybe you can avoid some of the mistakes I've made. And maybe you can have some of the fun I've had. Some of this is not appropriate for young ears or weak stomachs, but I'd rather you hear all the gory details from me instead of some ex-wife's comedy act or the *E! True Hollywood Story*. That way when the other kids ask, "Who did your dad used to be?" you can say, "Actually it's a funny story. He was born in Ottumwa, Iowa, on March 6, 1959 . . ." Ottumwa, Iowa, was actually a literary hotbed. Richard Bach wrote *Jonathan Livingston Seagull* while living there (I went to school with his daughter; she still has my Bobby Sherman album) and another lady who lived there has written at least twenty Harlequin romances (some even had Fabio on the cover), so I've got a lot to live up to.

If I'm gonna write about my experiences, I gotta start with my childhood (all the best writers do this, too). The happiest memory of my life was my first birthday party. I don't know if I actually remember it, but I've seen the film and it looked like a lot of fun. I was sitting in my high chair covered in chocolate cake while my parents and their friends drank cocktails and danced. I've spent forty-two years trying to chase that feeling of euphoria, pure joy, and contentment. I've been around drunken relatives and eaten entire cakes since then, but it just wasn't the same.

The time that Scotty Potty swallowed the baby-sitter's hearing aid was pretty cool, too. Dad lined us up and gave us a stern lecture about swallowing other people's property. He kept saying, "Daisy, don't worry; we'll get it back." And she kept saying, "Huh?" It was a waiting game as the device wound its way through the two-year-old's intestinal tract. But Scotty finally did what he did best and we were once again a happy family. Then, after Daisy silently made her way into the icy Iowa night, Dad did something unbelievable. He, an adult, apologized. He apologized for blaming my sister and me for Scotty's crime. We cried. Dad didn't, of course, 'cause "he's a man, goddammit." I've never seen him cry and wouldn't want to, but I'll never forget The Apology. It was a life lesson that has stuck with me to this day. I didn't have the heart to tell him that I was the one who put the hearing aid in Scotty's mouth. That would have ruined our special moment.

Kindergarten was exciting. I made lots of friends that first fall after I told my teacher that I didn't have my crayons because they melted when my house burned to the ground. It was Halloween night and the pumpkin candle got too close to the curtains and now I was homeless. The other kids rallied around me.

They were suddenly nice to me. They brought me blankets and canned food. It was a dream come true. I almost wished it had really happened. My world came crashing down after the principal, Mr. Whittlesey, phoned my dad at work and offered his condolences. But I did make the paper. The story of "The Little Boy Who Told The Big Lie" is on page 1 of my scrapbook. I think that was my first foray into show business. It was also my first foray into getting paddled by "Mr. Whittlesticks." With Dad's consent I was paddled more than occasionally for other crimes and misdemeanors (eating paste and farting during quiet time; the paste was very gassy) throughout my grade school career. After I got famous, I went back to Anne G. Wilson Elementary School to talk to the kids. My first-grade teacher would not speak to me. She was still mad because I wrote *diarrhea* on the chalkboard almost thirty-five years ago. I will not be thanking her during my Oscar speech. The new principal said if I could bring Roseanne back with me (I sensed that if she wasn't available it was a deal breaker) they would have a special assembly for the "good kids." I told him that I'd rather fart with the bad ones. He didn't understand. I guess he never ate the paste.

Daddy, Did You Ever Have
a Real Mommy?

Yes, baby, I had a "real" mom for a while. I used to use the term a lot as a kid. Like, "My real mom is coming to visit next weekend and it's going to be great!" or, "I'll tell my real mom how mean you are and she'll let me move in with her." See, when parents divorce, as mine did when I was four, Lori was three, and Scotty was one, the missing parent takes on almost mythical status. This isn't fair to the remaining parent, the one that does all the parenting, but it's a good way to suppress the feeling of gut-wrenching abandonment.

In the sixties when there was a divorce, the mother always got the children. But when Jack and Linda parted company in 1963, it was not so cut-and-dried. Mom's drinking and general instability made Dad nervous, so a court had to decide. It was a long and expensive (for my grandparents) trial, and when it came to the day I was going to have to take the stand and tell the court where I wanted to live (i.e., who I liked better) Dad gave up. He did not want to put me through that. Mom won and the very next day she celebrated by stopping by my dad's office, giving him the keys to the house, and telling him, "The kids are there with a baby-sitter and they're all yours." Think *Kramer vs.*

13

Kramer. We must've been pretty rowdy during our twenty-four hours with Mom. Either that or she came to her senses.

I can't really say that I ever got to know my real mom all that well. She came in and out of my life occasionally and at holidays, but I can honestly say that I did not miss her chaos. My mom, Linda Kay Graham Arnold Paxton Purdon McCombs Heiford Collier (I know I'm missing one because there were seven), had many friends at the bars where she worked and played. She was always telling jokes and the young people called her Mom, which was ironic because the woman had absolutely no maternal instincts.

When she was sixteen she told my dad that she was pregnant (she had a lifelong aversion to the truth), so he dropped out of college and married her. She always told me that Dad was her favorite husband (quite an honor) and Dad, bless his heart, never said a bad word about the woman.

Mom was closest to my sister Lori. She'd say things to me like, "Too bad you're not doing as good as your sister; she just bought a new house and car and . . ." Mom and hubby number seven, Delmer the Cop (his dad's name was Elmer, swear to God, and he was the chief of police), actually worked (doing legitimate stuff) for Lori and her husband Floyd, the motorcycle gang leader, during the couple's glory years immediately before the DEA sent them to the federal penitentiary. By the way, the government confiscated their house and car and . . .

I guess it boils down to the simple fact that Mom and I just never hit it off. Nothing particular, just a personality thing. We were never comfortable around each other, unless we were both drunk. That's something we had in common. I remember once a guy came up to me at a football game and said, "Hi, Tom, I'm your new dad," and I'm like, "What happened to Bob?" It was at that moment that I vowed to be nothing like her.

So of course a few years later I was on her exact path. In 1989, when Roseanne and I were going to get married, Mom did a story in a tabloid about how bad a son I'd been. Not like my sister Lori, who by now owned an airplane in spite of the fact that she had no legal source of income. Mom also said that her bad son had not invited his mother to his wedding. But the truth is, the invitations hadn't even gone out and there was one with her name, whatever it was at the time, on it. In some strange way, I think she was jealous. I'm sure she was proud of me, but she wanted to be a performer and somehow I was living her dream. But the article was the final straw and she was uninvited. Unfortunately, we didn't talk after that.

She did call and leave supportive messages when I was in rehab, but I couldn't deal with calling her back. That would be surrendering and I was too ashamed of myself at the time. I kept tabs on her when she was in and out of the hospital. Calling the nurses and doctors. Her body, after years of abuse, was breaking down. Heart attacks, strokes, and then one day I got the call, the fax actually, from my brother Chris stating that "Linda has passed away."

When I read it I jumped up from the breakfast table and started running upstairs. I had to get away. I had to be alone. I had to think. "Oh, she was an old whore," Rosey said, trying to be shocking and funny, but all I could feel was a kind of sad relief. Selfish relief that I wouldn't have to worry about her messing with my life anymore, but mostly relief that she was finally at peace. She'd suffered enough.

I went to work that day and didn't tell anybody on *The Jackie Thomas Show* what had happened. We were reading a new script I'd never seen, and when I got to the place where my mother died I laughed. Somehow, she was still fucking with me. To the dismay of my sibling Lori, who was already in prison, I did not attend Mom's funeral. I had a show to do. But that weekend I flew back to Iowa by myself and went to her grave and read her a letter I'd written. The first part contained the things that I was angry about, and the second part was the things I was grateful to her for. The ironic thing was that both parts of the letter were the same. I was mad that she left me as a child, but I was also grateful because if she had not, my life would've been so much worse.

I thought about how hard my life had been as an alcoholic and how hard hers must've been, too. I thought about the shame she must've lived with, and I forgave her. I wished I'd been able to help her get sober. I wished I would've sucked up my pride and reached out more. But I knew that the greatest gift I could give to her now as my mother was for me to take care of myself and stay sober and live a long and happy life.

Mom's final husband, Delmer, who remarried a little too soon after the funeral, allowed me (with a small bribe) to move her remains to the cemetery where her parents are buried. I got her a nice new headstone and I put her maiden name on it. The name she had before her life got screwed up. Today she is an inspiration to me. They say that no alcoholic dies in vain, and I have the luxury of seeing my future if I don't follow The Path.

A month later we did an episode of *Roseanne* where her father dies. I put the letter that I read to my real mom in the script and Rosey read it to her dead father. She won an *Emmy* for that. Mom finally made it to the big time.

Daddy, Did You Ever Get
a New Mommy?

Yes and no, cutie pie. After a few years alone with my brother, sister, and me, my dad decided that it would be the best thing for all of us (especially my sister Lori, who was completely lacking in the feminine wiles; her ten years in prison and job at the meatpacking plant haven't helped things) if he went out and found us a new mommy. Who could blame him? He'd been a single father, raising three little kids, since he was twenty-three. Hell, I'm old enough to be his father now, which of course would make me my own grandpa. Anyway, because my dad was lazy, he set his sights on our hillbilly twenty-three-year-old next-door neighbor lady and her two younguns. Which was really disappointing for me, because I had seen the movie *Houseboat* and I wanted Sophia Loren to be my new mom. I also thought Cary Grant would make a pretty fine dad if the situation presented itself.

Next-door neighbor lady Ruth was none too thrilled, either, about having three heathens mixing it up with her whiny little Baptists, especially a smart-ass nine-year-old like me. But she loved my dad and figured that she could break me. She figured wrong. I would break *her*. I was wrong, too.

17

Now I tried to get along with her at first, because I loved my dad. Besides, I wanted a mother, but I was delusional as many kids are. I didn't remember my real mother being a mother that much, so I wanted my fantasy mother. Like the ones in the magazine ads, who are baking and hugging and kissing (I really liked the baking). I even tried calling Ruth Mom—Dad's idea—but I felt like such a phony and she wasn't buying it, either. So it was me against her, and she was a scrapper. She was a wiry little minx, almost five foot tall, ninety pounds tops, but with the heart of a barroom brawler. You always knew where you stood with Ruth, because she kept a chart on the refrigerator and every time your room wasn't organized or you mouthed off or you spoke up you received a check by your name (I was the Barry Bonds of the check mark). That made it very convenient for Dad. He'd walk in the door after a long day at work. She'd immediately lead him to the fridge and they'd add up the checks. She'd hand him his belt. They'd call me downstairs. Dad would do an extra underwear search (extra-padding rules were strictly enforced and punishable by extra lashes). Then the fun began.

Although I don't plan to ever spank my kids, I have to admit that there were times in my life that a beating was understandable. Like when I climbed the Memorial Park water tower across the street from our house. Most parents get a little upset when their offspring risk their lives for the sake of stupidity. So, when I was thirteen and I climbed the seventy-five-foot tower at two in the morning, I was crusin' for a brusin'. Not only was it pitch-black outside, but in order to get to the top I had to let go sixty-five feet up, fall backward, and grab the top rail that jutted out three feet around the base of the actual water tank. Then I had to pull my dangling ass up over the side. Getting down was even more screwed up. I shouldn't have been as surprised as I was the next morning when the park superintendent knocked on my parents' door. Probably had a lot to do with the fact that I'd painted my name on the side of the tower. So, you see, my punishment was deserved. Not only for my reckless endangerment but also for the fact that now the superintendent would no longer give my dad his weekly ten to twenty loaves of surplus day-old (month-old is more like it) bread the park's mangy ducks wouldn't eat. The glory days of "unlimited toast" were a thing of the past.

Ruth had some pretty fancy moves, too. I could deal with the punitive haircuts in the front yard and the mouths full of liquid dish soap, but I hated getting my mouse milked. It's not as sexy as it sounds. To get my "undivided attention," she would grab my hand and bend my pinkie inward, pushing my fingernail into the top of the back of my knuckle. Try it; it fucking hurts. It was a little trick she picked up from her own father, and I guess she wasn't ready to break the cycle. I also got whipped with a variety of instruments, sometimes "bare-assed," almost every day until I was twelve. Then one day I grabbed the big wooden spoon out of her hand, broke it over my knee, and said, "Never again." It never happened again. The next day, I was sent to live with my grandparents.

Ruth's brothers and sisters were an interesting bunch, too. They were a little wilder, a little louder, than my dad's and mom's. They argued a lot, and I listened and learned. ("Hey, Dad, what's a dirty whore?") But I found them fascinating. Especially Jack and Shirley Fry. Shirley, Ruth's sister, was about five-nine and Jack about four-nine. They were always nice to me even when Ruth wasn't. Especially when Ruth wasn't. They stood up for me. Damn, that felt good.

They've been married almost fifty years now. They were very young and a little immature when they tied the knot. Especially Jack. Shirley tells the tale of the day many years ago when Jack cruised by their house with his girlfriend, stopping out front and literally yelling, "Na, na, na-na, na!" Shirley, eight months pregnant with their first, comes bursting out the front door carrying her shotgun, but, before she can fire, she slips and falls down on the sidewalk. This causes Shirley to go into labor, which for all practical purposes ended Jack's date. Actually, it ended Jack's dating, period.

Jack, who was eight inches long at birth, has had a tough life, too. He's been burned, blown up, and crushed. Burned when a gasoline tank got away from him. Blown up to the ceiling of his gas station garage when a big old tractor tire exploded. Crushed when while working for the highway commission, he was thrown over the front of his steamroller, run over, and smashed into the ground. Somehow, after massive injuries (even for a little man), he survived it all.

Jack was also the one to tell the family secrets (maybe that's where I got it from). Through him I knew that Ruth's first husband was both a hard drinker and a scoundrel (I always liked the guy myself). But Jack's stories did help me to find a tiny little soft spot in my cold, cold heart for my stepmother. Anyone who walks in on her husband in bed with her sister (the "dirty whore") is gonna be a little testy. The fact that this affair produced a child, who I always thought was a cousin but was actually some sort of stepsister once removed, would make a woman a little on the crabby side, too.

In Ruth's defense, she was way better with the other children. She even had her own little day-care center for twenty-one years and she treated all of those kids like gold (now that really pissed me off!). For the past several years Ruth has done a wonderful job working with at-risk kids at a local grade school. Today I love my stepmother. It's the kind of love that Vietnam vets feel when after twenty-five years they go back to Saigon to visit the enemy. They realize that the enemy was just doing their job, they're not so different, and war is a hell that sucks for everybody involved.

Living with my grandparents was scary, too, for different reasons. The only naked woman I ever saw up close until I was sixteen was my grandma. I knew it was wrong, but every time she bent over to kiss me good night I looked down her nightgown at her massive knockers. I could not control myself. I hope I don't go to hell. Remind me to talk about my great-grandmother.

And while we're at it my Uncle Bob, my dad's only brother, is a fun-lovin' guy and a sixty-seven-year-old nudist (he even strips down and goes to that crazy-assed "Burning Man" rave out in the desert). But more important, he's got a fourteen-inch scrotum. I've seen it, and not just in his bike shorts. You'd see it, too, if you went to his house back in Cedar Rapids. You'd have to. That's the rules.

Daddy, Did You Ever Have a Real Funny, Funny Friend?

Sure I did, stinky. Everybody needs a Mo. A buddy you've known since you were a kid. A friend you can count on to get your back. A friend who keeps you grounded. A friend who is always more than happy to whip out his penis. I bet Hanks and Cruise had a friend like this. All guys have a friend like this. The one in the group who's not afraid of public exposure. He'll do anything for a laugh, as long as it involves his penis. The amazing thing is, our friends don't have to have huge equipment to be "the one," just a lot of guts. Mo has a nice package, but he's not even the largest in his own family. His little brother has the biggest wiener, and he's a lawyer. Talk about irony. I was a houseboy at the Tri Delta Sorority at the University of Iowa. Mo would come to the formals and pose for pictures with the ladies. After they were developed, the lovely Tri Delts would gather around the piano to gaze at the proofs; "I'll buy this one." "Tear it up; I look fat in that one." "Oh, look, it's Mary Jane, Mary Beth, Mary Lynn, and Mo." "Oh-my-God, that's not what I think it is, is it?" We were busting a gut in the kitchen. Funny, funny stuff. Believe it or not, Mo, who did not have a consistent set of choppers until he was thirty-eight (drunken trampoline accident in high school), is now gainfully employed and a happily married, loving father. But he still likes to please. If you ever need anything in Chicago, call Mo. Last year as I was at the Regency in New York City getting ready for our buddy Brownie's wedding, the hotel phone rang. On the line was a very passionate lady who insisted that I had to "make me come now." Since I figured that this was a joke or at least a setup of some sort by my girlfriend, I declined and turned the lady over to Mo. Mo likes dirty talk. But thank God for cell phones, because she was insatiable and it was an all-day affair. Finally culminating at the church during the wedding rehearsal, Mo is marching down the aisle and his phone rings. Before he even gets his bridesmaid to the altar, Mo's dirty talk ("Do you like it from behind, you dirty bitch?") had worked its magic. Once again he had satisfied another damsel in distress.

I wasn't always as good of a friend to Mo as I should have been. His dad, Big Jake, was the neighborhood badass (this was a long time ago; he's sober now). He was tough on his kids—especially Mo, but he spanked them all. He spanked us, too, and Dad couldn't do anything about it because Big Jake probably would spank him. Big Jake went to law school at Notre Dame. He loved the Fighting Irish. His house was full of green. His pants were green. His truck was green, with Notre Dame plates. Once while he was away, Mo took his life into his own hands after much peer pressure and threw a big party at Big Jake's house. Mo was a nervous wreck, scared shitless that someone would spill green beer on the green carpet or break some valuable Notre Dame memorabilia. Early in the evening Mo was horrified to see that I was wearing Big Jake's famed wool Irish derby: "Oh, God, please don't touch that. Dad will kill me."

That was all the information I needed. Cut to three hours later: Mo steps out on his back porch and spies Pat Kurtz (the toughest of all of our friends) and me urinating in Big Jake's famed wool Irish derby. I thought we were making a political statement

24

about Big Jake's treatment of our buddy Mo. But Mo was like (what's ten times worse than horrified?), "Oh-my-God! I've got to run away tonight!"

I told him not to worry—I'd get it dry-cleaned and it would be as good as new. Better even.

The next day, when I presented Mo with the newly laundered hat, he freaked. It had shrunk! It was now a mini-me version of the original dorky-looking lid. He considered burning his house down as a diversion. But instead he put the derby back on its perch, in the old man's closet, and sprinted to mass. The next morning Mo held his breath as his father donned his beloved derby, tugged on it, and left for work. It now looked like a yarmulke, but Big Jake was none the wiser and Mo lived to see another day.

Back in 1992 some producers came to Roseanne and me (actually they came to Roseanne, but I was there; I was always there) with a book written by Rita Mae Brown, Martina Navratilova's former love slave, titled *The Woman Who Loved Elvis*. They wanted to make a movie. The story took place in a small town, so "we" agreed to star in it if they could film it in Ottumwa, which was near our farm back in Iowa. This was especially exciting to me because this finally made me the big shot I've always dreamed of being in my hometown. My friends and family wanted to be in it. My grandma Dottie Arnold, who'd won several trophies as Best Actress from the Ottumwa Community Players, informed me that because of her past "thespianic achievements" she deserved a speaking part. Which was all well and good except for the fact that she had won these accolades before she was legally blind, and deaf. That was one long day of shooting. But the director, Mr. Bill Bixby of *Incredible Hulk* fame, was a patient man and we finally got the shot. At the wrap party I played a tape of her numerous outtakes and flub-ups. My family laughed until we cried. She cried, too. She was a little sensitive.

The townsfolk loved Bill Bixby. He dined on the good china

at my parents' house and posed for pictures. Unfortunately, according to my stepmother, my dad, "being the total jackass that he is, forgot to put film in the *gotdamn* camera and now Bill is dead, and there is not a *gotdamn* thing he can do about it." Dad wishes he were dead, too, because his humiliating screwup still gets thrown in his face on a weekly basis.

Bill Bixby had a zest for life and he loved making movies. One day we were shooting out on this country road and I was to ride my motorcycle down a hill past five cameras set up in various angles and locations in a cornfield. My "hero shot," Bill said. I was hidden behind a tree, and just before he rolled the cameras my buddy Mo gets a great idea. Wouldn't it be funny if he took off all of his clothes and rode the motorcycle down past the cameras and crew naked? "That's great, man. You've got to do it," I said.

Bixby yells, "Action!" and I wait, giggling to myself, for the applause and cheers. But they were not to be. I heard Bill yell, "Cut cameras! Destroy the film!" Mo, who sheepishly appeared back at my hiding spot, said that instead of laughing and praising his bravado, Bixby had in fact, run out of the field and tried to tackle his fat, naked ass. I went down to face Bill. He was pissed. "We're moving on. We aren't getting the shot because of that good-old-boy stunt."

I felt terrible. How could I be a hero with no "hero shot?" Mo felt bad, too. In all his years of public nudity this was by far the worst reaction from the fans, if you don't count the hot dog bun incident at the mall. Then, as we were packing up, I remembered that I was the executive producer and that I, in fact, had hired Bill Bixby. I summoned him to my trailer and we had it out. "I like to have fun when I work!" I screamed. "And if you don't like it, I will bring in someone who does!"

His reaction was completely unexpected. He cried. He told me he was sorry and that he was having a bad day.

"Don't worry about it," I graciously said. I hugged him as men do. He winced. I guess I could've been a little more sensitive. The warning signs were there earlier when I tapped him on the arm and he yelped. I believe he even said, "I'm having a bad day, Tom." But our drama made us closer, and the rest of the shoot was a breeze. Later I discovered why he was having such a bad day. That very morning he found out that not only was his cancer back, but he was experiencing some serious wife troubles. These facts haunt me to this day. But Mr. Bill Bixby was a forgiving man with a sense of humor. When he died he had a poster on his office wall from the movie. Not the official one but a special one featuring a fat naked Mo on the motorcycle.

Daddy, Was Your Family
Fun Like Ours?

Well, dear, fun was had, but not by all. My family was a yours, mine, and ours group of steps, halves, and wholes. We started out with Dad, Lori, and Scotty and me. When I was nine and a half we merged with Ruth and her little Johnny and Marla. Then we all added Chris and Mark. I don't consider my steps to be less than my wholes. Partly because we grew up side by side on Center Avenue but mostly because Dad treated everybody the same, the bastard.

The advantage to having a large family (seven kids, two parents) is that if one sibling goes away to prison for twenty or thirty years (Lori), another is a born-again Christian Bible beater (Johnny, thirty-nine) whose faith does not allow him to accept your Judaism (me) or another brother's homosexuality (Chris), and still another has antisocial behavior (Scotty) that probably stems back to his premature birth, when the incompetent doctor cut him during the cesarean, you've still got more than enough siblings (Marla, thirty-five; Chris, thirty-two; Mark, thirty) to share your life with.

I love my family; it's just that we're not all friends. That happens even in the finest of families. I have not had a real conver-

sation with Scotty in many, many years. At first, it was my doing.
I judged him. I hate it when abandoned kids abandon their own.
But I eventually realized that no amount of criticism would
change this sad situation and, if for no other reason than to
please my dad, I decided it would be for the best if I felt sorry
for Scotty. He has had a hard go of it in life. Lots harder than
me, and he never had the tools to dig himself out of it. Even if
he did, he probably would've sold them for beer money anyway.
I'm sure it must be annoying to have people coming up to you
in the bars asking about a famous brother that you don't talk to.
Wondering why you're not rich like him (little do they know).
But that still doesn't explain why he treats me with a sarcastic
aloofness that is usually reserved for someone you do *not* owe
money to. I understand that he is working and he and his wife,
Gidget, have a beautiful little baby. That's good enough for me.

Then there's Johnny, door-to-door messenger of God. It could
be worse. He could be a religious nut *and* in prison. But Johnny
(an actual red-haired stepchild) is probably just doing what he
believes he has to do to keep his marriage together. He and Little
Linda have been married seven years. This time. They were married seven years before. Then they broke up (God's will) and
Johnny moved in with Big Linda (210 pounds to Johnny's 120
pounds) for seven years. Big Linda was tough. She used to sit
on the little man of the house until he "simmered down." We all
laughed. Hard.

I like Johnny. We have a video of a Thanksgiving dinner where
Johnny started choking on his turkey. He turned blue and hit
the floor, but we were laughing so hard that we couldn't catch
our breath, either. His real mother (Ruth) jumped in in the nick
of time to save his heaven-bound ass. She always liked him better. But it takes all kinds and to this day I can't say that I enjoy
anything more than Johnny's and my theological debates in the
grease pit at the Lube King where he assistant-manages. Espe-

cially if gay Chris is with me. Nothing like an angry queen to drive away customers.

I didn't know that my brother Chris was gay until he was twenty-four. I just thought he was odd, uptight, perhaps asexual, but a gay guy from Iowa . . . no way. First of all, he was a Young Republican. Second, he has slept with at least one skank. It was about two years BG (Before Gay) that I noticed Chris had never had a girlfriend. He had plenty of girl "friends," but I was genuinely concerned that my little brother was a twenty-two-year-old virgin. So I mocked him mercilessly. He swore he had in fact boned down with one of my sister Lori's sleazy runnin' mates. "I got ten grand says you're lying," I wagered.

When we shook hands I kinda felt sorry for him, having so much shame that he had to lie to his big brother and all. A big brother who had lost his virginity at sixteen to lovely Ann, fourteen and also a virgin, or so I thought until afterward as we sat in the afterglow (and the wet spot) in the front seat of my Caprice and she cooed, "Duh ya wan me to go back on the pill . . . Tim?"

Ann and I romanced on every dirt road in Wapello County until she dumped me for her new stepbrother three days before my prom. "I guess I could still go with ya if ya really, really wanned," she snarled. But I foolishly still had some pride and I went stag with the other losers after making twenty-five phone calls and getting turned down by the twenty-five best-looking women who didn't have a date to the 1977 Ottumwa High School Prom, only seventy-two short hours away. Women who now all certainly regret their decision, since I would've had another humorous story to share and their name would've appeared prominently in a slow-selling celebrity tell-all.

So Chris gives me the name of this gal and I call her up to verify and she is sweet as ever: "Yeah, I screwed him, Lori made me, wasn't very good, though, don't think he'd done it before." I'd be gay, too. But that didn't matter, because once was enough and a bet is a bet. So I gave my bitched-up little bro $10,000. Well, actually I gave him $2,500 and $7,500 worth of art. A Norman Rockwell painting I'd bought from a scary homeless guy.

I was at my parents' and this sweaty, panicky man knocked on the door (that happens a lot when I'm back at home). He said that he was broke, no gas in his car, no food for his kids, and that he wanted to sell me his final possession, a Rockwell masterpiece, for the bargain price of $15,000. Well, I took one look at those hungry kids in the backseat of his beat-up Rambler and, thinking with my heart instead of my head, said, "I'll give you seventy-five hundred dollars, take it or leave it; either way you've got to get the hell out of here," and we had a deal. A deal that was good for the both of us. You can support a family of five for about ten years in Iowa for $7,500 and I got a hell of a bargain on a Rockwell.

At least I thought it was a Rockwell until I noticed the snow-covered landscape was signed by a guy named Fred something. Then I started getting suspicious. I didn't remember Norman Rockwell working with chalk and I turned over the picture and I saw a tag that said, and I swear to God this is true, Roseanne will back me up on this,—well, she might not because she hates me so much—but Chris was there and the price tag said: "Goodwill, seventy-five cents."

So I gave Chris the "Rockwell" and we were even. And, yes, he was pissed. But I, being older, bigger, and meaner, made the rules. I'd always told Chris that if he was gay he could tell me and that I wouldn't judge him, because I'm hip and I work in Hollywood and everybody's gay here. So when I actually found out, I was surprised by my reaction. I was filming *McHale's Navy* in Mexico and he and his special friend came to visit. I liked Jason. He was nice and had by far the better personality of the two (best abs also).

Anyway, they were sitting there in their matching bike shorts and Jason puts his hairy, toned man leg over Chris's and Chris doesn't jump up and call him a big fag or anything. He doesn't even flinch. They've done this before. As cool and liberal as I am, I gotta admit that my heart sank. I felt bad because I knew that gay guys have a harder life than the rest of us. Especially gay guys from Iowa. But I supported them.

I called my parents and they were surprisingly cool, too. It wasn't a big deal. Maybe because their love for their son overruled any petty prejudices they may have had or maybe it was because they knew their six other spawns were breeders. Chris's boyfriend now is black (ten-inch Tony) and Chris loves to show him off at my folks' back in Iowa. I think he's trying to kill them. But Jason was Chris's first love and so of course, this being my family, he died tragically. He had a seizure and drowned in the shower. Chris found him. He was only twenty-one. Nice guy, too, darn it.

Marla is the best-looking Arnold sibling. Not much to brag about, but I'm proud to say that she is an inner-city grade school teacher in Kansas City with two cute kids. Apart from occasionally having one drink too many on weekends (remember, I am Mr. Sobriety), Marla does a damn good job. She's been a single parent since we had an intervention for her former husband (a liquor salesman, ironically) and he chose not to go to rehab but instead to abandon his family in favor of disappearing to Florida with a skanky barmaid. He has only been heard from recently because of that state's fine deadbeat dad laws.

Marla and I have always stayed in touch, except for a nine-month period before which one of her boyfriends beat her up in front of her kids and put her in the hospital. Of course I called and threatened his life and of course she went back to him for nine months, hence the nine-month Tom Arnold Communication Blackout. But, like I say, she's doing well now.

Mark is the youngest and he is an excellent single father with a handsome ten-year-old son, Spencer. I blame myself for Mark's divorce since I was the one who made him get married. His girlfriend, Wendy, was pregnant, so I told him to get her and

come out to my trailer. I had a judge standing by and we officially un-bastardized Spencer in front of God and the guy that
filled my propane tank. But Mark brought out the worst in
Wendy and he's got the scars to prove it. We Arnold men love
the crazy ones.

Mark is a real nice guy and he worked for me at my farm for
a while. We had a hundred head of cattle and a hundred horses
and Mark was especially cut out for this line of work because
he has a thing about poop. Most people are disgusted by it, but
Mark embraced it. He liked working with it. He thought it was
funny. I guess that's why he always put it on the doorknobs on
my other brothers' houses.

Mark, Johnny, Chris, and my big buddy Mike Sporer all lived
on our farm. It was a beautiful place, 2,500 acres outside Eldon,
Iowa. Our property went right up to the actual house that Grant
Wood used in his famous painting *American Gothic* (I would've
given $15,000 for that one). My brothers and Mike oversaw the
crops and broke the horses. The horses belonged to sister Lori
before she got busted. They were quarter horses, not the best
for riding, and the U.S. government gave them to me because
they, too, like their original owners, had serious drug problems
(to their credit, the horses did win a lot of races).

Good times were had by all as my brothers climbed atop each
jonesing filly, one after the other, only to be bucked off, horse-
kicked, and slammed into the steel fence. Broken ribs and
chipped teeth later, it was still one of the funniest things I've
ever seen in my life. Until they added paint guns to the mix.
Then people really started getting hurt. Still was funny, though.

After the farm closed, Mark took a series of jobs, including
male stripping, where sadly, because of a combination of Coke-
bottle-thick glasses and back acne, he was let go. At private
parties he and his roommate, Mike Ball (that is seriously his
name), performed a duo act that opened with some impressive
hillbilly calisthenics and closed with Mike (Maverick) and Mark

(Goose) paying hairy-assed homage to the "coolest fuckin' movie of all time," *Top Gun.*

Mike, who also worked for me at the farm as a very creative handyman, would only respond to instructions if you called him by his idol's name, (TV's) MacGyver. Once, in an effort to join us on vacation in Hawaii on a farmhand's salary, MacGyver built a man-sized crate complete with a blanket and a cooler of beer for the five-to-seven-day freight-only semitractor-trailer truck cargo plane ride. Fortunately, we talked him down. The thought of a stinky dead male stripper showing up in a box at my and Roseanne's cabana in Maui outweighed whatever hilarious-future-story-to-tell-our-grandkids value we could think of.

Mike was an old hand at the flesh game and told us that he was so well endowed (eleven inches), the ladies called him the White N-word. He didn't actually say "N-word," because we lived in a part of the country where the politically correct folk had just started using the term *colored.* One night we were out at the Pop-a-Top and MacGyver was on a roll and he said that he wanted us to get some girls to pull down his shorts so he could show off his new Budweiser beer thong. A couple of local love-lies obliged and he's groovin' on the dance floor and I'm thinking about his claims of greatness and I pick up the microphone and announce that I had $100 for the first person who could rip off Mike's banana hammock.

The music stopped and everybody froze. Especially Mike, as he got down in a martial arts position that I assume was inspired by the great Richard Dean Anderson (TV's MacGyver). "Please, Tom, don't," Mike begged, but he had nothing to worry about, because this crowd of factory workers and parolees could not be bought for $100. No mob mentality here. I admired that, but the second I said, "Two hundred dollars," three men, north, east, and west, took flight—one still had his cigarette dangling from his mouth—and the Anheuser-Busch Spring Break Party G-string lost its G.

I was told that there is a reflex animals have when under attack that causes their reproductive organs to take shelter. I was told that by Mike. Little Mike on this day. No more racial epithets connected to his good name. After the laughter died down, Mike forgave me and we made our way out of the joint, which by now had erupted into a bitchin' fistfight as three hammered manual laborers resorted to violence, clearly from the frustration brought on by the stress of trying to figure out just how in the hell you could possibly divide 200 by 3.

Brother Mark's foray into the world of strip was not for naught, as he met the new love of his life, Misty Moonlight (stage name). My family first met Misty at Chills and Thrills, Ottumwa's only and probably the skuzziest strip joint on the planet. When the local Baptists (Johnny, Little Linda, and company) tried to shut the place down, the management started handing out sketchpads and pencils at the door. Strip clubs were illegal; artists' studios were not. As we sat at our table, pencils in hand, Mark scurried around the stage picking up wrinkled one-dollar bills that had been hurled at his sweetie when suddenly Misty did a naked back flip off the stage and tumbled, crotch-first, into my dad's face. Nice.

Of course when Mark and Misty crashed and burned, big brother Tom was there to pick up the pieces. To this day, Mark sends me a check for $100 every month—well, almost every month—as payment on the $17,000 credit card bill he and Ms. Moonlight had accumulated. I confiscated the big-screen TV, but I could never figure out how to repossess the boob jobs. Two of them! One huge and one fucking *Guinness*. Apart from a slight resentment I have against Mark for the other $25,000 I wasted on him for rehab, I'm happy to say that Mark, his new girlfriend (we affectionately call her the Badger), and Spencer live somewhat happily somewhere in Iowa.

Daddy, I Want to Be Just Like You Were

Thanks, partner, but I was hoping for so much more than that for you. I want you to follow in the footsteps of the great Toms: Cruise, Hanks, Clancy, Jefferson, even Selleck. When I look at my life from ages sixteen through thirty I'm amazed. I really should be dead, murdered, or in prison. Actually, dead, murdered in prison. If I ever murdered anyone now, it would be me then. Warning to young people: Drinking too much and taking lots of drugs can be . . . a lot of fun! Especially if you don't think about the constant threat of little things like sudden death, jail, and generally ruining your own life and the lives of everyone that cares about you. I'd tell you all the different drugs I did, but it'll be a lot easier to name the ones I didn't do. I didn't do heroin and ecstasy. Not that I was above it. I just ran out of time.

I've been clean and sober since December 10, 1989. I know it's hard to believe that when you see my leg shaking and multiple twitches on television. I know it's distracting and obnoxious, but when you consider that part of my attraction to cocaine was the fact that it calmed me down, I think I've earned the right.

When I was a kid and was diagnosed with what would be

called ADHD (Attention Deficit Hyperactive Disorder) my parents were relieved because now there was an actual medical explanation for my intolerable behavior. And better yet, they could now legally drug me into submission. Who could blame them? When the oldest of five kids with two more on the way has this much energy and the uncontrollable urge to speak his mind, he must be stopped before he contaminates the others. Besides, how else do you get any kid to stand in the corner for three hours nose to the wall with a red ass and a mouth full of dish soap because he "disrespected an elder."

So Ritalin it was. Ritalin is a form of speed that when given to hyper children acts as a depressant. Some hyper adults react the same way to uppers, hence: Tom Arnold, cokehead. I hated Ritalin. I hated the way it made me feel; I didn't like to calm down. I liked a little chaos. Chaos was my friend. Besides, I thought I had a better chance to make friends at school if I had a personality. So I refused to partake. But I had to eat sometime, and that's how they got me.

I'd be thinking about a million things, eating my cereal, and my brain would suddenly feel warm and I would know that they'd done me in one more time. Sometimes my parents got creative. I'd open up my bologna sandwich and the little Ritalin pills would be forming a smiling face, but usually it was just crushed up and sprinkled on my Wheaties.

When I was a kid, you didn't miss any meals. Breakfast was at 7:30 A.M., lunch at noon, and dinner at 5:30 P.M., and if you were late, tough shit. And there was no snacking or, as Stepmom called it, stealing food. The kitchen cabinets were locked, and for good reason. We had limited food and unlimited appetites.

I remember once Dad caught me eating a can of tuna in between meals. So of course he completely flipped out. "I don't understand you, Tommy. Are you crazy?" he yelled.

"Yeah, Dad, I'm tuna crazy; please help me!"

A couple sprinkles of Ritalin and I was staring out the windows remorsing for my crimes. And to think I would one day grow up and buy that man a luxurious purple conversion van.

The first time I drank a beer was on the football field behind my house when I was eight. Eddie was my dad's age, but his days were free and he always had time to play sports with us kids. Eddie's nights were free, too. Eddie was fun. Eddie was a drunk. Why couldn't my dad be more like Eddie? Anyway, Eddie let me chug one of his Old Milwaukees. Eddie was so fuckin' cool and he always gave us each a shiny new dime. This was in the old days when you could get a big-ass candy bar (they call it supersized now) for a dime. One day, we went to Eddie's house to see how he was doing (we wanted our shiny new dimes) and his wife answered the door and invited us in. Eddie's house was full of people and they were partying, but it was a different kind of party. Everybody was dressed in black. Especially Eddie, who was stretched out in a shiny new coffin in the middle of the living (now that's ironic) room.

With Eddie's warm brew a thing of the past, I didn't start drinking heavily until I was fourteen. I was the drummer in a country rock band with my fifth stepfather, Kenny, and his bass-playing buddy, Dave. Except for a couple of amphetamines-and-alcohol-induced rages, Kenny was good to me.

And except for the time I caught him making out after a show with a pretty hot (especially for Melrose, Iowa) lady, I'd say Kenny was darn good to my mom, too. I was sad when she dumped him for Delmer, son of Elmer.

Back to the band. Kenny was good to me, but Dave was better. Dave let me drink with him. Dave always imposed a three-tall-boy limit because "we have a show to do at the VFW, for God sakes." I loved being drunk. I felt good about myself and I could talk to Dave about anything: "Do girls like big penises? . . . So a big penis would be like what, four, five inches?"

If I could've kept it to three tall boys I'd still be drinking today (and talking to bass player/welders about penises). But three turned into four and four turned into fourteen. I got arrested for the first time when I was sixteen. Possession of a traffic control device. I asked if I was going to jail and one of the cops said, "No, we're taking you home so you can tell your dad what you did and he can deal with you!" I begged them to take me to jail.

Dad was generally not a violent man (although I could bring it out in him), but I feared him anyway. That's why when he bought a new skill saw and told me to "stay the hell away from it" I did. Until he went to the office; then I immediately sprinted down to his "work area" in the basement, turned the saw on, grabbed the first board I could find, and cut the end of my finger off. I was more frightened of my dad's reaction than the bone sticking out of my left hand's "pointin' finger." Another note for fathers: Your sons will *always* find your guns and the ammo to fire them up with, even if the ammo's in a lockbox in a hidden compartment above the ceiling of your closet.

So I wrapped my injured hand in a dirty rag and went about my day. That night at dinner, Dad became suspicious because I did not have both elbows on the table as usual. "Let me see your hand, Tommy," he demanded. So I showed him my hand. "The other hand, dammit." I slowly raised my blood-soaked southpaw. "If you've been into my paint, you're grounded until school starts!" I was trying to imagine my punishment for my much graver crime when I threw in my chips and started crying. My fellow diners' confusion turned to horror as I unwrapped my hand and flashed my bloody digit. All was well (except for my career as a classical guitarist) until we got back from the emergency room. I was banned from the basement for life, and apart from school, I did not leave my room until the snow flew.

Another time, I was selling Thin Mints door-to-door to pay my way to Y camp and this old lady's crazy-assed dog attacks me and rips my new, and only, pair of red, white, and blue striped bell-bottoms. I went home and told Dad, and of course he didn't believe me. I couldn't really blame him; I had a 75:25 lies-to-truth ratio at the time. So Dad said, "Show me this dog." I took him over to crazy dog lady's house and he knocked on her door and was still giving me the "I know you're lying and you're gonna get an ass whuppin'" stare when she opened her front door just a crack and Cujo burst out and took a major chunk out of Daddy Dearest's thigh. I laughed hard, even as the dog turned his attention back to me and chased my giggling butt the six blocks home.

Anyway, when the cops woke my dad up that night after my first arrest and he heard "possession" he had a shit fit. When I explained that I'd "only" stolen a stop sign from a major intersection, he was relieved. Me and six of my drunkest friends were cutting doughnuts in Wildwood Park with said traffic control device sticking out the back window of our GMC Travelall (great party mobile). That was the first time I mouthed off to a cop. That was also the first time I had a .45-caliber standard-issue police revolver cocked and jammed up to the side of my head. At least I was smart enough not to get caught driving drunk. Not yet anyway. That would have to wait until next year.

The day I turned sixteen, I got my driver's license and my first car. A mint-condition '68 Chevy Caprice. I bought it with all my corn detasseling and country rock drumming money. And since I worked hard for my money I was gonna take care of this beautiful piece of machinery, but as I was backing out of the car lot I ran into a pop machine and dented the quarter panel. Fuck it, now the car was a battering ram. Soon I was entertaining guests by knocking over klingons (klingons are those barricades with flashing yellow lights that are placed in front of giant holes in the road or missing sewer covers, etc.). We'd spot one, start making the *Jaws* theme song sound, and I'd open my door and knock the flashing bastard over.

I became an American hero one night after drinking six bottles of Boone's Farm Strawberry Hill wine (is it really wine?) and stealing a bunch of flags. My friends and I were bored as usual, so we drove around town and if we saw a flag we shimmied up the pole and snatched it. No reason. Just shits and giggles. We took the Mexican flag from the Fiesta Cantina and a Confederate flag from some idiot's house (we weren't hip to the flag's racist connotations back then; we just didn't like the particularly greasy redneck who flew it), but mostly we took American flags. Fifty-two of them over a three-night period. The police had been notified and were looking for us. But each night we got braver and dumber, and finally, on the last one, we hit the jackpot, which rested atop the well-lit pole in front of the cop shop.

Now the authorities were really pissed. The police chief told the newspaper that felony theft charges awaited the flag thieves. Seven to ten years in Fort Madison State Prison. This was almost starting not to be funny. Almost. But now I needed to fight back, so I called Dan Palen, radio's "Voice of Southeast Iowa." Using a subtle Foghorn Leghorn southern accent, I explained on air that we had committed our crimes to protest those who left their American flags out at night and in the rain. "Ah say, they disrespected Old Glory, son, and America, not to mention Alabama and Puerto Vallarta."

Dan got it. He said that we were good, brave Americans. I told him that we would give him the flags back as long as he guaranteed the flags' safety. Including the Mexican flag. The Rebel flag was already in the Des Moines River.

So the next day we carefully folded the flags and boxed them and dropped them down by the train station. We tipped off Dan and he went live on air: "I'm just arriving at the location and I can see something, it's a crudely wrapped package [sorry, Dan], could be a bomb, the police are opening it anyway, and it's . . . the flags! The flag thieves kept their words and they taught us all a lesson. They are truly American heroes! They should step forward and publicly accept our praise." I don't think so, Dan; your kind words were thanks enough.

42

I should've been in jail lots of times, but I wasn't locked up overnight until Christmas Eve of my eighteenth year. I'd broken Dennis Redmon's dubious record of thirty-four by knocking down thirty-five Ottumwa stop signs (I think we only had about forty total). I was cruising home minding my own business when suddenly out of nowhere a squad car cut in front of me and ran me off the road. Those assholes! Turns out they'd been following me for six miles, but how was I to know with my windows covered with ice and my eight-track blasting Ted Nugent's "Snakeskin Cowboy"? Officer Allen asked me out of what was left of my Caprice. He asked if I'd been drinking and driving around town knocking down stop signs. Of course I said no. Then he led me to the front of my car and showed me the stop sign dangling from my bumper.

Needless to say, and deservedly so, I was roughed up and taken to jail. This was my first incredibly serious criminal-type situation. I'd been previously charged with reckless driving after running head-on into a highway patrol car (sober, shockingly), but I won that case because the elderly county attorney got flustered when he had trouble reenacting the crash because the little toy cars wouldn't stick to his fancy new magnet board.

As I sat in jail I knew one thing: I never wanted to be sitting in jail again. Being in jail is not fun. They take away your dignity, your freedom. Your shoestrings. In other words, it's a lot like, for lack of any kind of humorous metaphor, being in jail. So I made a big decision. I would never again knock down, steal, or run over any stop signs. Or, for that matter, any traffic control devices period. In hindsight, I probably could've taken a little look at the drinking, since I woke up a lot of mornings with bitchin' hangovers, having no idea what had happened the night before. Until I realized that I was missing something important. You know, like shoes, pants, teeth, an eyebrow, that sorta thing.

I lived with my mom and Kenny for a year and a half in high school. (I moved in so I could eat snacks and grow my hair over my ears.) Mom's rules were kinda lax: "beers in the fridge"; "if you wanna screw your girlfriend, bring her over, it's OK, because we're going to Missouri for a month." But after a psychotic incident involving Mom, Stepdad, whiskey, and diet pills, I ran for my life back to Dad's.

Dad's rules were a lot tougher and they included "be in by midnight or sleep in your car." I only slept in my car once and Dad snuck out at 4:00 A.M. and let me in. Good old Dad. Every other time, I was smart enough to crawl through a window. I never remembered much until the next day when Dad would pull me aside and let me know that I knocked down "sixty of your mother's [give it up, Dad] prized plants." She loved those darn plants. Or Dad would let me know I left the oven or deep fryer on. All night. Harmless stuff like that.

Drunks are dangerous, even teenage ones. Once I came home drunk and made myself an apple butter sandwich. Yum! I knew I was breaking the food laws, but I also knew it was a risk worth taking. Until the next morning when I snuck to the fridge to get some more of that delicious apple butter and discovered that what I thought to be a jar of apple butter was actually an apple butter jar full of bacon grease. The fact that I was too drunk to tell the difference five hours earlier did not, for some reason, disturb me in the least. The fact that I considered eating another sandwich just like it did. I complain about my parents, but let's just say I wasn't the perfect child.

Like when they went on their first vacation. We never had family vacations when I was young and now, at seventeen, I was deemed too large to fit in the AMC Pacer station wagon with the eight other smaller Arnolds. So, I had to stay at my grandparents' because I wasn't trusted in my own house. I was deeply hurt. But after tricking the dear sweet neighbor lady into loaning me the emergency key, I was back in and the party started. My parents had promised to come home on Sunday, but without clearing any of this with me, they cut their trip short and showed up unannounced Saturday night and ruined the best party I ever had. One hundred of the coolest people from Ottumwa High were drinking, smoking, urinating on Ruth's prized plants, or just lounging around nude in my parent's bed.

My dad (Mr. Buzzkill) walks in and physically throws everybody out. Thank God I wasn't there. I called in from a beer run and Ruth answered, "Tommy, get home now!" Fuck that. I showed up four days later and everything I owned, stereo, record albums, my clear Fibes drum kit, was baking in the sun in the field behind my soon-to-be-former home. My apologies went unaccepted, and I started searching for a place to call my own. I laid low for a couple of weeks, except for one really weird night when I think someone slipped something funky into my drink, because instead of making a left to go up to my room, I made a right, took off my clothes, and was just getting comfortable when I felt my Dad's hairy leg.

I was sickened. "Dad, what the hell are you doing here?" I whispered in the darkness. Then when I felt my stepmom's hairy leg I sprang up, turned on the light, and yelled, "Why are you two in my bed?" I began to notice that my room looked different, flower wallpaper, no Shannon Tweed *Playboy* poster. "Oh, sorry, guys, go back to sleep. Show's over." Dad escorted me to my bed. The next day they put a lock on their door and I moved out.

I thought that if I only drank and didn't do drugs I'd be fine. Drug addicts were scumbags, greasers, and, worst of all, hippies. I was . . . Well, I wasn't a jock because being a jock would indicate that one's interest in sports was greater than one's interest in going to keggers. I wasn't a preppy, because I didn't study and couldn't afford the clothes. Wasn't a soc' because I didn't belong to any clubs, groups, or organizations. I wasn't any of these things because, quite frankly, none of those people liked me. In fact, the only ones who liked me were the scum-bag, greaser hippies. Finally I surrendered. If you can't beat 'em, join 'em.

So immediately after high school, I smoked pot for the first time, gave up my dream of being a stockbroker/lawyer, and went to work at the Hormel meatpacking plant. Soon I decided that with my future prospects being what they were, it was probably OK if I took a little LSD. Cut to New Year's Eve. I'm wasted on anisette and acid, which I'd ingested earlier at my grandparents' house. And I'm in jail after being hauled away from my own New Year's Eve party. Now I'm facing second-offense drunk driving and twelve more hours of panic and paranoia in the county drunk tank. And most of all, I was missing my own fucking party!

Acid, even the best acid, is not a good jail high. It's like being in a prison inside of a jail. During my brief moments of clarity, I swore to God (who actually appeared as my cellmate) that I'd never, ever do acid again. I swore I'd stick to mushrooms, equally as weird but, when mixed with lots of Jack Daniel's, a much shorter, sweeter psychotic event. I did try a hit of acid a few years later while in college at the University of Iowa. Actually, it was two hits, might've been three, but I was so drunk I kept forgetting if I'd taken as much as my buddies. And I always had to take as much as my buddies.

Truth be told, I always had to take more than my buddies. My college roommates, who hated me (all my roommates always hated me), were having their Christmas celebration and I hadn't received my invitation when I walked up to our front porch and peered into the living room window. Norman fucking Rockwell would've been pleased. Those four snobs were sitting around the beautifully dressed (flashing lights and what appeared to be a real live angel on top) Christmas tree, exchanging beautifully wrapped (and brightly colored) gifts. With my nose stuck to the frozen glass, I felt like Tiny Tom, and those Scrooges were not going to get away with this.

46

In a flash, I dashed in, grabbed the tree, and sprinted outside and heaved it onto Gilbert Street. My freaked-out drug buddies said that because the tree had a long extension cord the lights didn't go out until it crashed on top of my neighbor's Karmann Ghia (not a very good Iowa winter car, if you ask me). Then we danced off into the night.

The next day I had to go home. I was a little embarrassed, so I had my buddy Mo call my roomies and tell them that apparently someone had spiked my Diet Coke with PCP and I shouldn't be held responsible for my actions. Nice try, Mo, but they weren't buying it and I was greeted by the angriest mob of sociology majors in the Big Ten Conference. Everything in my room had been destroyed. My clock, my books, my bong ("No, goddammit, not my frickin' bong!"). Then the pummeling began. I knew I deserved some of it, but one roommate was especially punitive and I begged her to stop.

The thought of having my ass kicked by a chick haunted me for years and years until one day I received a letter from her. She was doing well, had gotten a great job, and was living in San Francisco. Oh, and, by the way, she was now a man. I felt better, redeemed about my ass whipping, then horrified. *Hey, wait a minute*, I thought, *Didn't we hook up?* I wrote Francine/Frank back and said that I was grateful we could put the ugly past behind us. Behind us . . . that's right; we did hook up.

In my twenties I dated a few really nice women. I always had long-term girlfriends because I always wanted to get married and have the perfect family I never had. Funny how things work out.

Jan was my college sweetheart. She was the youngest of seventeen, believe it or not, Catholic kids (fifteen girls, two boys) who all grew up in a three-bedroom, one-bathroom (indoors) farmhouse. I got very close to Jan's family because when we went to visit for the holidays I spent many nights in bed sandwiched between daughters fifteen, sixteen, and seventeen. Nothing weird, just being practical. There was no heating upstairs and you needed the bodies, although if you'd thrown daughter fourteen or twelve in there it might've been a different story.

Jan was very sweet and I was very immature. Her roommate got engaged one day and I felt bad for Jan, so I went down and got her an engagement ring of her own. She accepted it, skeptically, but gave it back the next day because she didn't want to rush. I also think it probably had something to do with Jan catching me making out with her roommate's best friend at our engagement kegger. Looking back, I'm sure Jan is grateful for our time together and considers her years with me to be a valuable life lesson. She went on to a long and award-winning career as a special ed teacher.

The first time I got engaged I was eighteen and chiseling heads at the Hormel meatpacking plant. She was seventeen and only a high school junior. But this being Iowa and she being from Missouri, she was ready. I asked her to marry me because I knew I couldn't work at that hellhole and not have a mortgage to face and family to support. I was old enough. My mom married my dad at sixteen, and my future convict sister, Lori, married at fourteen, and she wasn't even knocked up. Long story, my mom was involved. Actually, it's not that long. Lori's loser boyfriend, Bob, was twenty-two. Mom gave Lori three choices: Break up with him. "But I'm in love." Have him arrested. "But I'm in love." Or they could all get drunk and drive to Missouri and get hitched. Bingo! After a brief, tumultuous marriage (Bob was pretty handy with his fists) Lori's beloved died in his bed in a mysterious fire. I don't know what happened, and I don't want to know, because there is no statute of limitations. Anyway, *I* was about to get married when one day, as I was cutting a dead pig's ears off with a dull saw, I had a moment of clarity. I realized I had to get out of there and if I got married I'd be gutting hogs and pulling leaf lard for the rest of my life. I also would never have fingernails (I'll talk about the world's worst job later) and, more important, I'd never move to Hollywood, become a star, and be best friends with Robin Williams (my recurring dream). So instead of calling off the wedding like a real man, I used my alcoholism to try to drive her away. That way she'd dump me and I'd feel abandoned (see "real mother"). This was always my pattern and it only got easier when I became a drug addict. But she was a gamer, and a drunk, too. She told me she was pregnant. This was long before I knew I had an extremely low sperm count (turns out it's bad if your testicles do not descend until you're four), so I was stuck and I said, as romantically as possible, "Fuck it, let's get hitched." I even asked her father's permission to take her away from the only home she'd ever known. He seemed relieved. Two months before the wedding, a miracle happened. She met Franky, a drummer from Moberly, Missouri (I was a drummer, too, but he was way better). She dumped me, told me she was never pregnant, and married him. I'm sure she's been divorced at least as much as I have.

Daddy, Did You Ever Do
Real Hard Work?

I used to, kiddo. This is where Daddy shined. The worst job at Hormel was pulling the fat out of the insides of the hog's ribs. You do it in one upward motion with both hands, and it tears your fingernails off and cuts the sides of your fingers. That was just one of the cool jobs I did. I also drove hogs. If a pig couldn't go up the chute to be electrocuted *humanely*, you know, a broken leg or something, I'd *humanely* shoot it in the head and put it out of its misery. Then I'd hang it out in the back and *humanely* cut its throat. One day, it was lunchtime and there were six of them, all crippled. You're supposed to do them one at a time, hang them up to get the blood out ASAP, or the meat tastes gamy, but I was hungry, so I thought what the hell. I shot them all, left them sitting on the dock, and went to eat my pork fritters. The government guy came back and condemned them. We had to throw them away. That's how I got the nickname Gunner. That's also the first time they tried to fire me. Thank God for the union. They did actually disarm me and put me in the chitlin line. I had to squeeze the shit out of chitlins for six months because of that. Then I got a good job chiseling heads. The heads would come by on this conveyor stuck to metal stakes, staring me in the face. My job was to remove the temple meat. Good stuff. But for fun I used to cut the scalp off and put it on my helmet as I was working so I would have big pig ears. Everybody loved it, except the government guy. When he wasn't looking we'd throw things at one another—pig knuckles, blood, guts, and big green abscesses. Good times.

Because I was young and stupid I'd do anything to impress the old-timers at the plant. This is why I "red-boned" Judy Martz. She was a nice lady and we didn't have too many gals on the kill floor. I was a slob, but her white uniform was always spotless. So everybody thought it would be funny if I dipped a ham bone in blood, snuck up behind her, and gave her a big red streak up the crack of her ass (red bone). The crowd went crazy and Judy was pissed. So was the government guy. She put down her steel mesh gloves and waddled out. That night I heard her husband wanted to kick my ass behind the union hall, but I guess he thought better of it. Maybe he heard of my rep. I was undefeated behind the union hall.

Meatpacking is hard work and, much like filmmaking, really, really boring. You have to make your own fun, and the old guys liked to start trouble. One would come up to me and say, "I heard Cubbage bad-mouthing you; he says you're a puss."

"Fuck him; he's the puss."

Then he goes over to Cubbage: "Arnold says you're a fag."

"He can suck my dick; I'm not a fag. He's the fucking fag."

And so on. Next thing you know it's "duke city." Since everybody has really sharp knives, fighting inside the plant was impractical. So after we clocked out we'd all head for the union hall, where we'd throw two or three punches. Somebody would give up. "You're the better man tonight." Then we'd all pile in our shiny new pickups, go to the nearest happy hour, and drink shots until the bar closed. Five-thirty the next morning back at work was a little rough, but I didn't care because I was living the good life.

During my college years I was incarcerated a few more times and I hadn't even tried my drug of choice yet. Interfering with official acts is the charge when you try to stop a police officer from carrying out his duties. I discovered that included every thing from something simple, like trying to outrun a cop on a 100cc minibike because you don't have a license, to kicking the same cop in the back of the head because he wouldn't let you button up your pants before he sucker punched you while you were taking a leak after you gave him the finger because he kicked you out of Henry's Hamburgers for drinking a beer. Little tip: If you are stupid enough to commit a crime, be smart enough to flee the scene.

I know that you can never win a fight with a cop, especially a big old redneck small-town Iowa one. But when I lifted my boot and gave Big Bruce that little love tap to the melon, I sure felt empowered. I bet he also felt empowered when he whipped the squad car over and pulverized my sorry handcuffed-behind-my-back ass.

A week later, Iowa's football team was playing in the Peach Bowl in Atlanta. After the worst seventeen-hour car ride of my life, with six other guys and a trash bag full of urine, I get to my seat at the stadium and guess who is sitting next to me? That's right, Big Brucey. But no fists would fly tonight because we were off the clock and in neutral territory. We smiled and shook hands, as men do, because we both knew that we would live to fight another day. Little did I know then, when that day came I would be in the nude.

Public nudity is usually real funny or real sick. With me it was a little bit of both. Streaking was popular on the coasts, in the early seventies, but it finally reared its ugly head in my home-town in 1980. I was working nights at the meatpacking plant and going to Indian Hills Community College during the day. See, even then I had big dreams and I knew that George A. Hormel Company insisted on a college degree before I'd even have a shot at moving up from pig killer to foreman. The foremen are the pussies in the clean white coats who stoically stand by with their thumbs up their asses doing nothing, which is why I dreamed of becoming a foreman.

Since I worked eight to twelve hours a day and took a full load of classes, I had little or no time for my hobbies, getting drunk and getting drunker. The fallout from this loss of artistic freedom was staggering. I made the honor roll.

To me the most important aspect of college is social. The opportunity to meet and mix with people from other countries, cultures, religions, ethnicities, and have sex with them. So when the big summer bash was announced I knew I had to be there. Problem was it was on a work night. The solution was simple and familiar—call in sick to work. Because I was a union man (I initially joined the union because I thought that there would be a lot of strikes) I could not be fired without plenty of prov-ocation. We had the three-strikes rule and I always had two strikes. Which is why I'd have to be a little careful with my most recent outbreak of chronic absenteeism. The party was a so-phisticated soiree with enlightening and informative tales of global American oppression. So after consuming a gallon of Ev-erclear and powdered Gatorade, we headed back to the dorm.

But it was still early, so I said to my nouveau socially aware buddies, "Why don't we streak through the old folks home?" And we did. It was so much fun. Then I said, "Hell, let's go to Mr. Quick's [a fast-food emporium]." I was pushing our luck. We ran in wearing only our shirts over our heads and jumped up on the tables. Scared the hell out of everybody. Unfortunately, the cops were waiting for us. Mo, Mike Sporer, and I jumped into our car to put our shorts back on. Three naked fat guys rubbing up against one another in the backseat of a Chevette was too much for me to bear. A crowd was gathering, so I stepped out to put my clothes on like a decent human being. I figured the cops would have a good laugh and send us on our way. I figured wrong.

Officer Allen grabbed me in the roughest possible manner (it felt rough, but then again, everything feels a little rougher when you're nude) and handcuffed my arms behind my back. He didn't let me put my shorts on, either. I'm in the middle of Main Street on a chilly night and people are driving by honking. I prayed this would be funny one day. Then the copper put me in the squad car and says, "You're a pervert."

I went, "*I'm* a pervert? Give me a fucking towel or something." Even a washcloth would've been more than enough.

So I got taken to jail and thrown in the cold steel drunk tank. Suddenly I didn't even feel drunk. The other guy in there was, though, and he said, "What are you in for?" and I was still naked, so I told him, "Murder, motherfucker."

Now, since it was only 10:30 P.M. and I worked the 11 to 7, I was not too concerned, because I'd always call in sick around 10:59. But my one phone call allowed was an important one. Once I got the other convicts to stop screaming profanities, I made my move: "Yes, Tom Arnold here, Kill Floor. I'm real sick, gotta stomachache."

"Where does it hurt, Tom?"

"Well, it's my stomach, so all over." *Click.*

I was golden until they read about the previous night's escapades in the paper. Front page—it was a small town. No union could have saved me. Three years of seniority down the drain. There would be no gold-plated Spam-faced watch for me, as there had been for my grandpa, who had worked in the packinghouse for fifty years.

This was not how my family envisioned the ending of my meatpacking career. "That's a shame. That was the best job you'll ever have, Tommy," my not-so-proud grandma said.

My dad, Mr. Conservative Industrial Engineer (he once devised that a 1,000-sheet roll of toilet paper should last a family of four six months, two squares a day per man, minus times at grandma's) had to bail me out. The next morning he came to my cell and said, "The sheriff says you ran naked through Jefferson Square Manor. That's sick, but I want to hear your side of it."

"Dad, he's lying."

"I thought so," Dad said as he handed me my underwear. To this day we have never talked about it. I was naked in front of him again recently (we aren't one of those liberal naked-type families). We were at a spa, and I booked us some massages. We both had to be nude in this little room. I was worried about how my body (penis) looked. He didn't seem to mind how his (penis) looked. He must be getting senile.

Back to the story. Without my job there was no way I could continue to pay for my top-notch community college education (i.e., my ticket to the big time). I didn't even consider asking my folks for help. They would've laughed. I never even got an allowance my whole life, and I was a slave to those people. We lived like animals. We didn't have air-conditioning, there were five boys in one room upstairs, and we only had two bathrooms for nine people. So, we lived in a simple white house with yellow streaks down the side. Anyway, I'm broke and tuition is due so I came up with my first legitimate scam. I'd walk twenty-one miles in my underwear, in the middle of the winter, and people could pledge money. I wasn't curing cancer, but I needed some schoolin'. It was an incredibly stupid idea, so of course it caught on like wildfire. Before I knew it, the whole town was involved and I had $3,000. Then reporters from all over the country were calling. I was in the *New York Times* and the *National Enquirer*! Show business! Now all I had to do was walk the twenty-one miles from Albia to Ottumwa in my too-tight satin boxers in windy nine-degree weather.

The morning of the walk was brutal. The kickoff party and chugging contest the night before had caused me incredible physiological discomfort. But, as is my pattern, I had to pick myself up and carry on. It's a good thing, too, because the highway was lined with "well-wishers." Some people threw bottles at me, but most just wanted to see if I would die. Several mentally challenged students who lived in the dorm with me (my crew) rode in the lead van. Of course Mo was there, too, exposing himself to oncoming traffic. My grandma Dottie even showed up in a full-length mink stole and high heels to walk with me and share some of my glory. She lasted about six seconds. The hills were icy and steep, but five hours later I saw the "Ottumwa Is a Beautiful Place" sign and knew that there was a keg at the park with my name on it. Apart from a few blisters, numbness in my genital region that lives on today, and severe skin rash where my thighs mutilated each other, I was as good as new. Best of all, I was kinda famous! Oh yeah, and I had some money for school.

One night when I was out and about, I saw a sign that changed my life. Not the sign outside of the Jailhouse, Ottumwa's premiere and only disco, that read "5-cent Beer Night." I saw that sign every night. What I saw was impossible. I saw Andy Kaufman. The great comedian/wrestler and star of *Taxi* was standing on the sidewalk outside the bar in my hometown.

This wasn't my first brush with greatness. I'd met Festus from *Gunsmoke* at a telethon in the sixties. But Andy was one of my idols and I had to talk to him. He was nice, if a little hurried, maybe because he was surrounded by ten touring female oil wrestlers but probably because I was bugging him. He said he was staying at the Maharishi International University down the road in Fairfield and he'd heard about the oil wrestling.

Andy arrived at the Coliseum as the show was ending and the heavyweight champion was making one final attempt to pull her sticky thong out of her sticky ass (unassisted). Andy paid the gals to extend their performance so that he could participate. Then my new idol took the whole audience, two hundred-fifty strong, over to Happy Joe's (home of the world's best taco pizza). This was my kind of guy, and it struck me if someone from Hollywood could wind up in Ottumwa, Iowa, covered in hot chick oil maybe someone from Ottumwa, Iowa, could wind up in Hollywood. Covered in hot chick oil. Me even!

Back to reality. I was still having philosophical problems with this whole "alcohol and drug addiction is a disease" crap when I got arrested a third time for drunk driving. My explanation to the highway patrolman who'd so rudely awakened me at the intersection of Main Street and Dodge in Iowa City, that "I had to drive because my buddies are even more fucked up than I am" fell on deaf ears. I got ten days in the Johnson County Jail. Not my favorite spring break.

My cellmate this time was a Vietnam vet, exposed to Agent Orange. This exposure had given him a condition I can only describe as perpetual boil syndrome. He was a busy man. Lots of pickin', probin', and poppin'. I decided to turn lemons into lemonade and fasted for my entire sentence.

My first experience with cocaine, in 1984, was probably like most people's. I was at a party and somebody gave me some. I snorted it, didn't know what the big deal was, went out in a blizzard to find a cash machine, drew all of mine and my girlfriend's money out of the bank, and bought some more cocaine. Wet, lather, rinse, repeat.

I'd left the University of Iowa the year before with $100 and a Hefty bag full of clothes to seek fame and fortune via the comedy stage. After performing some old but filthy jokes I'd heard from my mom or read in *Hustler* at Open Mike Night at UI's Student Union, I'd taken the halfhearted response of fellow alcoholic undergrads to indicate that I had a big future as a stand-up comedian. I bragged to all that I'd be on *The David Letterman Show* in six months (actually, I did get on *Letterman* in exactly six months—and nine years later). I'd just completed my fourth year of college, and at the rate I was collecting credits, I figured I'd get my B.A. in General Studies around the turn of the century. Besides, I had a job waiting for me at the Minneapolis Comedy Cabaret. The owner, a traveling comic, passed through Iowa and killed every night when he put on these funny black glasses with these crazy-looking eyeballs that bounced around on miniature Slinkys (we were easily amused). He said if I was ever in the Twin Cities he'd have a job for me. Rent was past due, so that was all the coaxing I needed to hear, and thirty-nine dollars' worth of bus tickets later (my driver's license was permanently revoked, not that I could afford wheels anyway), I showed up at the club and by God if he didn't keep his word. I had a job, doing comedy, in a real comedy club. I was officially a stand-up comic! If I'd had a phone, friends, or a place to live I would've called people and bragged.

I asked the owner if he knew of any cheap apartments in the area. I figured that since I'd be working at the club I might as well live within walking distance. He figured that I could broaden my apartment search since my job was for only this one weekend and paid fifteen dollars. Ouch! But . . . I was still a paid stand-up comedian. Not unlike Richard Pryor or Robin Williams or the guy with the funny eyeball glasses.

After my five-minute set the other comics critiqued me and I learned a couple of valuable lessons: (1) Comics hate it when you do jokes before they go on that you stole from them when they performed last month in Iowa. (2) Comics are bitter, small-minded twits. Since none of my new peers had roommate potential, I, Hefty bag in hand, headed for the nearest bar, Williams Pub. Here is where I would find some friendly faces, a room for rent, a real job, and over one hundred beers from various countries around the globe. Not to mention fifty-year-old scotch and all the free peanuts and cocktail wienies a man could eat. Yes, this would be my home.

When I was a bar-back/bouncer at Williams Pub, the bartender, Val, and I had quite a system. We'd open up at 9:00 A.M., I'd have a couple Long Island Iced Teas, maybe a glass of fifty-year-old scotch from a bottle that I'd refill with fifty-day-old scotch, we'd entertain customers until there was enough money in the till to steal, and I'd go to McDonald's and buy us breakfast. On good days, there'd be enough for tanning beds and exercise class.

I had a little thing for Val, but she was in love with the bar manager from the fancy joint upstairs. Like me, he was a terrible alcoholic, but I couldn't tell right away because this guy was a different kind of alki. He dressed all preppy and neat and talked about his summer house on Block Island, but Ivy League Guy was a drooler. One drink and saliva literally cascaded out of the corners of his speech-slurring pie hole. I'd seen a lotta drunks in my day, sad drunks, happy drunks, angry drunks, but Ivy League Guy was my first drooler drunk. Yet beautiful Val, with the thick auburn hair and the pure, light, almost alabaster complexion (even after we tanned), could not get over this guy no matter how much I made fun of him. But Val survived. Now she's a beautiful soccer mom with three kids and a drool-free husband in Duluth. She, Susie (our cute-but-surly-when-drunk waitress), and I still get together every couple of years or every time I get married, whichever comes first.

Ironically, the woman who gave me my first line of coke also took me to my first 12-Step meeting. The reason I don't say "AA" is because, for one, the second *A* is anonymous and if I did that and you read this and then you read in the *National Enquirer* that I'd gone on a booze-fueled coke binge, you might think that AA doesn't work when in fact it is the most successful lifesaving nonorganization of the twentieth and twenty-first centuries.

It is perfect, but man is not. Especially this one. I'll be OK today, but who knows? Tomorrow somebody might say the wrong thing to me and *bam!* God grant me . . .

All better now. I loved cocaine. I felt powerful and interesting and, more important, you seemed that way, too. Plus, now I could drink more. Six margaritas and a gram of coke and *bam!* . . . I was sober. Comedy was my job, but cocaine was my life and cocaine was expensive. So I had to get two jobs, then three. Selling *Time/Life* books, toys, hoagies. And I had four comedy "managers." All drug dealers. Yes, the good old days . . .

In 1986 I got clean and sober for the first time. My girlfriend, Heidi, dumped me the only way she knew how. She cheated on me with the refrigerator repairman. I can't blame her. I was not a good boyfriend and she did go on to marry and cocreate with this fella, but at the time I was crushed. I showed up stinking drunk with a bunch of my buddies at Pepitos Mexican, where she was a waitress. I followed her from table to table trying to shame her into reconciliation. I was not a smooth operator even back then.

This was exactly the kind of behavior that made Heidi run from me in the first place. But I felt guilty. Deep down I knew it was my fault and I knew I'd forced her into this illicit tryst with Mr. Frigidaire, so I went to Plan B. I got sober. This would teach her. This would make her regret the day the freon ran low. I was proud, too, and told everybody. Her boss, Joe, was a comic, so he kept her apprised of the new and improved Tom.

I even cleaned my bedroom. Actually washed my sheets. (Note to men: Even dark blue sheets don't hide all stains.) I got a lot of support. The newspapers ran stories; "Local Comic Ends Drug Tailspin, Heads for Show Business High." Heidi eventually caved and stopped by my house one day. I showed her the new me. Sober, thinner, cleaner. I showed her my sheets. We were back and the sheets were ready when suddenly I had a weird feeling. A therapist might describe this as a conscience. I didn't understand why, but I couldn't do it. I somehow knew that Heidi would end up hurt, or at least disappointed, and I escorted her to her car. I guess I was confused.

Did I want her back or did I want to get even with the Maytag repairman? I'm glad that for the first time in a long time I did the right thing. I let her go. Of course years later, between my first and second marriages, we hooked up, but that didn't count because she was separated and I was famous.

I stayed clean for six months. My career was picking up. No more part-time jobs. I was everybody's hero. Then I met a girl. Not just any girl, Melanie was a singer in a popular band. Beautiful, sexy, talented, way too good for me. I was a wreck. I knew that I was in over my head, but there wasn't a damn thing I could do about it. My friends couldn't believe that Melanie and I were actually going out. Neither could I. Whether out of insecurity or stupidity or an overdose of lust I was back, headfirst, headlong, into drugs.

I hooked up with all my old "managers." Took them down to see Melanie sing. "I can't believe she's with you, Tom!"

"Me neither, got a bump for your buddy?"

Of course, after a few months this love affair crashed and burned, with Melanie disconnecting her phone and me reduced to a whimpering, sniveling pussy. Looking back, some might say that she was using me to get away from her husband, but I kinda think she had the good foresight to see what kind of person I could become. I eventually moved on. Although for two years I took every date I had down to see Melanie play. I guess I was hoping that if they saw how hot Melanie was they might give me a chance. That's the same reason I carried around a skinny picture of myself in my billfold.

My final arrest (if you don't count punching out paparazzi at LAX, and who would?) was during the Melanie period, and I attribute this one to lack of drugs. I'd done a crazy-ass show in Rochester and on the way home stopped by McDonald's. After a verbal spat with the pregnant manager—"Oh, my God, how the hell did that happen?"—I was asked to leave sans Big Macs.

I was urinating on the McDonald's Kiddie Land seesaw when the squad car pulled up: "Hey, what the hell are you doing?"

So I'm like, "Wow, isn't it obvious, I'm making a cocktail; you want one?" See, if I'd just had some cocaine to mix with my gin and tonics, I would've been fine. Right.

Nightsticks and handcuffs later, I'm in jail and the authorities, having reviewed my file, decided that a thirty-day mental evaluation was in order. Which might've been true, but I was leaving the next day for L.A. for the first and biggest break of my career. I was gonna play Roseanne Barr's husband in her HBO special. I was so fucked. But, once again, God was looking out for me. I called the best lawyer in Minneapolis, who, shockingly, was a fan, and he called a judge on the golf course and, amazingly, I got sprung! If that had not happened, though a thorough psychological inventory would have been helpful, I most undoubtedly would not be writing this book. Well, I may have been writing a book, but it wouldn't have a happy ending and my reading audience would have been limited to my cold-called teammates at the Time/Life Book Building.

In spite of my self-destructive setbacks, my career was starting to move in 1987. I appeared on an HBO special and a Showtime special (to this day I can't watch it because I looked like I'd been on a five-day bender, which of course I had). The producer tried to sell me the footage after I got famous for an exorbitant fee, but I passed. I wasn't too concerned about it ending up on a "best of" compilation. Besides, it's an excellent reminder of where I was, how far I've come, and where I could be in a heartbeat if I screwed up.

But my biggest score of all was winning the Twin Cities Comedy Competition and $2,500. Hell, I could have used that money to move to L.A., if I hadn't already owed that and more to the club owner who ran the contest. Some suggested that he had to let me win, it was the only way he was going to get his money back. I don't know. Still got the plaque, though. But the most amazing thing about that whole deal was that I won the contest being me.

When I started out in comedy I did old jokes. Then a very funny and unusual comic named Joel Hodgeson told me that I had to have a hook. Something original. I loved Joel's act. He talked in a real monotone and had all these crazy ironic props. So I came up with my own original hook. I talked in a monotone and had these crazy ironic props. And I had goldfish. Trained goldfish. They did tricks and stunts. One did an impression of the pope. One was a sword swallower. One rode a motorcycle through a ring of fire. I became the "goldfish guy." Joel came and saw my act and I asked him what he thought and he said he liked it because it was like looking in a mirror. I thought he was complimenting me. He thought I was ripping him off.

So out with the monotone and in with the crazy drunk wired guy, which was a lot easier to pull off. Though it was harder on the fish. Sword swallowing is a dangerous game if your master has shaky hands, and that dechlorinated water gets a little icy when the boss forgets you're in the trunk while he's smoking crack in his "manager's" attic. So by the time I won the contest I'd given up the fish. People were amazed that I could do it on my own, but there were even bigger fish to fry.

I met Roseanne in 1983. I was an ignorant young mullet-headed twenty-three-year-old and she was a thirty-year-old Denver housewife with three (found out later in the *National Enquirer* it was four) kids. I was to be her opening act at the Comedy Gallery. I remember the exact moment we met. Scott Hansen, club owner, MC, and 700-pound man, brought me up to her at the bar and said, "Roseanne, Tom, I think you guys are really gonna like each other." Then he said something about not doing any fat jokes about him because his family was in the audience. So after he introduced me and I pulled on the curtain and said, "Hey, Scott, I think you left your pants up here," Roseanne was smitten.

Then I watched her act and I'd never seen anything like it, especially from a woman, no offense. She was tough and funny and smart. We became fast friends. We toured a little together and we partied a lot, but then she went home to her family and mellowed out and I went home and partied harder.

Roseanne offered me a writing job on her new TV show in 1988. Earlier she had offered me the husband role on *Roseanne*, immediately after which I called my hometown newspaper and bragged of my upcoming starring role produced by the guys that did *The Cosby Show*, Carsey/Werner. Needless to say, I was a little disappointed to read that some nobody named John Goodman got the part. Turns out it came down to the fact that he was a damn fine, brilliant even, actor and I was insane for even thinking I could breathe the same air as a man of his ilk. It still gives me shivers to think that all those talented producers had to line up one day and humor Roseanne with my audition.

But God bless her and anyway, this writing job was a dream come true. Roseanne came back to Minneapolis for my going-away shows. The house was packed with "managers" for my triumphant finale. My new fiancée, Denise, who was moving to L.A. with me (actually, I was moving with her; she owned everything), was a hairstylist and offered to do Roseanne's. Rosey was concerned that I was not moving out alone. I didn't figure out why she'd even care until later.

While getting styled, Roseanne asked Denise what I was like in bed. Somehow Denise took this the wrong way (women!), and when Rosey took the stage she looked like the bride of Frankenstein. And Frankenstein she was. Suddenly she was very cold to me, and she left on a bad note. Denise and I loaded up Denise's stuff in Denise's car and departed a couple of days later. In Albuquerque, we pulled over to a rest stop and I called my new boss to check in.

Rosey was weird. She said she'd thought about it, and she decided I shouldn't move out. I explained that we'd given up our homes in Minnesota and had already rented a beautiful two-bedroom in Van Nuys. Besides, how could I write on her show from Minneapolis? Then she dropped a bomb. I would not be writing on her show. What had I ever done besides write jokes for her? I had no experience with television scripts. No shit, but this was a kinda bad time to figure that out!

I hung up the phone with no job, no prospects. I'd just left town a hero and was fucked. So was Denise. I broke her the bad news and she was amazingly calm. "Don't you get it, Tom? She's in love with you!"

I argued, "How can you say that she's in love with me? I just told you how mean she was." Boy, did I have a lot to learn about women.

But Denise was a champ. She said she'd get a job and that if Roseanne saw talent in me, everybody else would, too. Denise had a lot to learn about Hollywood.

We got to town and Denise immediately got a job at Jerry's Deli in Studio City (home of the world's finest carrot cake) and I picked up a few one-nighters around Southern Cal. Then, as Roseanne always had in the past when we had a disagreement, she called and wanted to meet. She apologized for freezing me out, and even though I could not write on her show, I could write some jokes for her stand-up act and warm up her TV show's studio audience. It was a bone, and I gladly took it. Writing the act was fine, but I was the worst audience warm-up guy in the history of television. They let me go after two shows. Thank God.

On Denise's and my first day in L.A. we went out to have a couple of drinks to celebrate our new financially futureless life together and wouldn't you know it, the first man I talked to at the bar was a "manager" in waiting. We exchanged numbers and before I knew it, I was buying cocaine at one-fourth the price I'd paid in Minneapolis. How could I not buy it? How could I not buy it in quantity? I went from buying half-grams to quarter-pounds.

Denise had no idea that my "going-away show's" money was going away so fast. My excuse to myself was that I needed coke to write. Since I loved Denise, I needed to protect her, so I kept it to myself, but she wasn't stupid. Nobody had that many bloody noses. Thank God she had a job to go to so I could inhale my drugs in peace.

It got even scarier. I still didn't have a driver's license and I'd have to drive home from a show in San Juan Capistrano or San Luis Obispo or somewhere at 2:00 A.M. totally screwed up, hallucinating from the cocaine and lack of sleep. I'd see imaginary animals and people walking out in front of me.

I'd slam on the brakes time after time. Eventually, I learned to drive through the hallucinations. How stupid is that? Shit! Man, I should've been shot! By now Denise had had enough of my crap. She threatened to leave many times, threw my clothes out on the driveway (come to think of it, maybe she was trying to get *me* to leave). But I could always get her back. Finally, she came to her senses and moved in with a friend.

I remember being sad and more than a little embarrassed when Denise took our engagement ring back to the jewelry store along with all the other stuff I'd bought for her on *her* credit, guaranteeing to pay when I got my writing job. Months after we broke up, I called Denise and asked if she'd loan me her car to drive to a gig. She agreed to because I told her I was clean. When she picked it up a couple days later (I promised to "bring it right back") she found cocaine everywhere (I was a sloppy snorter). Denise wrote me a note and instead of ragging on me as she had every right to do, she said that she still loved me and she prayed I would take care of myself. That is how I remember Denise. With charity. A couple of years later, I paid off her bills, helped straighten her credit out, and gave her the money to open up her own salon back in Minnesota. It was the least I could do.

But now it was 1989, Denise was gone, and my drug problem was escalating. I tried to clean up, go to meetings, hang with sober people. Even got thirty days two or three times, but I'd always go back. In March, Roseanne informed me that she wanted to be more than friends. I was honestly surprised. I'd loved her as a friend for a long time. I told her that if we were gonna do it, we'd have to do it all the way. So we did.

It was a crazy time. The tabloids were on our tails. She was America's favorite mom, filing for a divorce after sixteen years of marriage and three kids to, according to the story, leave it all behind for this young no-name comedian (one actually called me a boy toy; I liked that one).

We brought a lot of the trouble on ourselves. Roseanne had a longtime relationship with the *National Enquirer*. She said that she knew she'd made it big when a sweet little heartwarming, rags-to-riches story about her miraculous rise to stardom appeared in the tabloid. But they turned on her. Lots of stars try to manipulate the press, especially the tabloid press, and I can tell you from firsthand experience you always get bit on the ass.

My first official brush with yellow journalism appeared in the *Enquirer* in March of '89. Rosey had said to me many times that she had to get out of her marriage for reasons that are better left in *her* book. She asked me to help, so I leaked a story about us dating. When she read it, she flipped. "Who would do such a thing?" she screamed.

"I have no idea," I said. Now I was confused, and I became even more confused when a check for $1,500 from the tabloid appeared in my mailbox.

I knew I couldn't tell Rosey, and I was never in a million years going to cash the check. That would be selling my soul, and my soul was not for sale. Not for $1,500 anyway. So I tore up the check and tried to go about my business. Unfortunately, I had no business and when another check came and I was out of drugs I did the unthinkable. I can understand screwing for drugs or stealing for drugs, maybe even killing for drugs, but selling stories about your relationship to a tabloid for drugs? Now that's just plain wrong.

I'd hit an all-time low, which of course made me want to take even more drugs. I finally started that writing job, so I had "ethical" drug money now. But my low-down dirty little secret came back to haunt me a couple years later when the editor of the *National Enquirer* went on *Geraldo* and ratted me out. Whatever happened to protecting your fucking sources? Have they no integrity? I had to come clean with Rosey, and she said she understood and that she could let it go. But as all men know, women do not let anything go. It was just added to the file of my misdeeds and hurtful comments that was opened up every time I called her on her bad behavior. Like all men, I also had a list of my good deeds that I would spit out in rapid-fire self-defense. But since I didn't have the magic, "Yeah, but remember when I took a bullet for you," or even, "When I met you, you had nothing," I always lost the battle of the lists. Note to men: Use caution with those lists, because they can backfire. I remember one argument with a girlfriend that went a little like this: Me: "How can you leave? I was always there for you! Remember when you lost your job? I was there. Remember when you broke your leg? I was there. Remember when your grandma died? I was there!" Her: "I know; you're *bad luck!!!*"

So since you're only as sick as your secrets, I was getting sicker by the minute. I was newly engaged, working the job of my dreams, and snorting a half-ounce of coke a day. I was a busy man! But I was making this all kinda work until Roseanne insisted that I give up the bright lights and sirens of Van Nuys for the swimming pools and movie stars of Beverly Hills, 90210. I didn't want to do it and I had a valid excuse. My car, a 1975 Chrysler Imperial, would not make it up the hill and over Mulholland. So I figured it would be more practical if I stayed in the San Fernando Valley where the studio was.

I don't blame the car. For six hundred bucks I was lucky it had wheels. My car budget was a little thin after I bought Rosey a $30,000 engagement ring. (Not to brag, but that was the least expensive engagement ring I've bought in the last thirteen years.) But Rosey was relentless, so I filled up the trunk and headed for Beverly—Glen, that is. She didn't believe that I really had car problems so she followed me, and it's a good thing, because my car stalled seven times up that hill. When I hit stall number eight, I abandoned ship, climbed in Rosey's Mercedes, and we were off to paradise.

But along with my new life of luxury came a new life of responsibilities. Jake, Jennifer, and Jessica. Rosey's kids. And Rosey's kids, much like herself, were not the kinda kids you could ignore and everything would be all right. They needed love and attention and adult supervision. We had so much in common. Now I really had to keep my drug use on the DL. Every day I got the kids up to go to school, which was a battle because Rosey had never made them go to school. Even a cokehead knows kids need rules and structure. More on that later.

I knew these kids were in trouble. So was I, because this parenting stuff is some serious shit. I'd been struggling since I'd been hospitalized in the spring with some sort of nasal hemorrhage. Rosey had found me in a bad and bloody way at my apartment and checked me into my first rehab. Four days out of thirty later my nose had stopped bleeding and I talked Rosey into checking me out early with my promise of some good lovin'. Of course, the disappointing results of this promise made it on her "list." But a couple days later as I was cleaning up my place, I found a stash that I'd obviously hidden from myself or from the "whisper copters" that I believed flew over my apartment and listened to all my ramblings. And like all self-disrespecting drug addicts I believed that this gift from God must be put to bad use.

But things had to change; there were children involved. I was usually good when they were around, but the minute they went to their fathers', it was business as usual. One advantage to having a family around is that if your fiancée finds your drugs, you can always deny it and blame the kids. That is, if you are the lowest form of human life. Which I was. But you gotta believe that I tried. I tried so fucking hard to keep it together. I was not handling the pressure of fame once removed, and as dumb as it sounds, having too much messes with your head if you don't have your priorities straight.

The worst part about the whole thing was the lies to Rosey. She suspected and I denied. She knew the truth and I convinced her otherwise. But the signs were so obvious. I was fine for a couple weeks; then I wouldn't sleep for four days. I'd tell her it was allergies. I'd tell her it was stress. I'd tell her anything to protect my disease, because I knew if she knew how sick I was she couldn't possibly love me. Nobody could.

We'd set January 20, 1990, as our wedding date and had rented the Ambassador Hotel, home of the Coconut Grove Night Club, for our ceremony and reception. This was a famous old Hollywood landmark, and ours would be the final event held there. Three months out, I started to get concerned. I believed that I could stop using, but the clock was ticking. The other *Roseanne* writers wrote a part for me on the show. I would play Arnie, Dan's (John Goodman) friend who stops by the house and gives Rosey a kiss.

At the time, I was not the most popular man in the writers' room. Partly because of how I got my job and partly because of the job I was doing. I had my moments, but I was a little, shall we say, unfocused. I was on a roll the week we were shooting my big network debut and was not doing well in rehearsals. I'm sure I was driving big John Goodman crazy. But in my defense, I *was* crazy. I had no timing and I was hearing voices. Those things will slow even the finest actor down.

Finally, on the night before our final run-through, the producers and the director pulled Roseanne aside and said that I couldn't do it and they wanted to cast someone else. They told her that I would humiliate me, her, and everybody else. She asked them to give me one more chance the following morning. That night I flushed my drugs and she went to work on me. We did the scenes twenty times each and she gave me the best acting tip I'd ever gotten. I was having trouble entering a room because of my lack of confidence. She said, "When you walk in the door, show me your dick." She meant it figuratively, I think, but that in my opinion is the key to acting with confidence.

The next day all the naysayers lined up for the run-through and they were impressed, surprised, and possibly a little saddened because I pulled it off. Thank God, because if I'd been replaced on my fiancée's show in front of everybody, I would have never acted again. I never did even try to act on drugs again. But now it was November, Thanksgiving, and I was still using. Roseanne was really on to me. She asked if I needed help. "Why would I? I'm clean. If you really loved me you'd believe me." I was a dog.

December rolled around and so did I and it finally hit me. I could not stop and I couldn't tell anybody, because it would fuck up everything. This was the first time in my life that I knew I was going to die. I'd had lots of other moments—lying in bed sweating with painful heart palpitations, picking up the phone to call 911, chugging bottles of 100-proof schnapps to try to mellow me out—but this was the first time *I knew*. And Roseanne finally knew, too.

It's 3:00 A.M. December 9, 1989. I was in my usual stupor, driving around Benedict Canyon, afraid to go home and face the music. When I finally got the guts to go home (i.e., I was out of drugs), I couldn't get in our gate because I couldn't remember my code. And the code was my birth date. So I called the house and I saw Rosey's car heading down our drive. The gate opened and I dreaded what was next. She was going to yell at me, probably hit me, and accuse me of being on drugs and it's going to be very, very ugly. She pulled up, got out of her car, walked up to me, and didn't yell, didn't punch . . . she just hugged me real hard and said that she wanted me to come home.

I was blown away. I felt that through the haze. I had a moment of clarity. Somebody knew the truth and still loved me. This is how I like to remember Roseanne. With gratitude. The next day, she asked me to tell her the whole truth and by God if I didn't try to lie again. But she said she was done. We were done and I was moving out. I knew she meant it this time, so it finally happened.

I hit bottom and I told her the truth. That I couldn't stop, I could not control this, and I knew I would be dead soon. The next morning I called a cab and checked myself into New Beginnings at the Century City Hospital, and I have not done drugs or alcohol since. My first night in I was watching the news and learned that because of my cocaine problem our wedding had been canceled and I had been fired from the show. I went in for Roseanne and for my job and the press, but I stayed in for me.

On my eighth day in rehab I had my spiritual awakening. I was finally feeling physically and emotionally good, and every other time I'd felt this way, I'd pick up the phone and order more drugs. But this time was different. I decided that I liked feeling good and I deserved to be sober, if not for me, then for Little Tommy.

I asked my parents to fly out from Iowa for my final rehab therapy session. This was going to be a tough one for all of us because I needed to confront them on some of the ugliness of my chaotic childhood. The risk was that they could say that it never happened. That all their "punishments" fit my crimes. Then I wouldn't have a family anymore. But the session was amazing. Dad and Ruth both took responsibility. They both said that they were sorry. They thought they were doing the right thing, but they just got carried away at times. That was more than good enough for me.

Suddenly Roseanne burst into the room. She started yelling at me in front of my parents. Something like, "Hurry up, goddammit; we have to take the kids to dinner!" At that moment, I learned an all-new level of humiliation. Later she apologized. She said she was just jealous that she couldn't do it with her own parents. Now I felt sorry for her.

On January 20, 1990, three days after I got out of rehab, Roseanne and I got married. Not at the Coconut Grove with six hundred guests but in our living room, with the few friends and family who didn't think we were out of our minds.

Dad, I Hope You Never, Ever Drink or Do Drugs Again, Ever!

I hope not, too, honey, and I'll be OK as long as I work really hard at it. They say that the key to working a good program of sobriety is that you have to give it away to keep it. In other words, you have to help others. This can really suck. It is oftentimes frustrating work because you're dealing with some of the most dishonest and manipulative people on the planet, alcoholics and drug addicts, like me. But when you help people who are struggling and they actually do get it, you get a sense of fulfillment that is far greater than anything charitable you could do that would be covered by *Access Hollywood*.

That's the key to anonymous programs. The world doesn't know the good or bad you do. That's why it's the purest form of service. That's also why I recommend it to other celebrities who are trying to find their sense of self. This is also true with young people. A lot of addict kids I talk to come from wonderful, very wealthy families where you'd assume they'd have a perfect life, without a care in the world. And that's the problem. They have no responsibilities, so they only have to care about themselves, and that gets pretty hollow. When you don't have to make your bed or clean your room or mow the neighbors' yards to earn a little walking-around money, I think you lose touch.

A little volunteering or just helping the less fortunate is good. Then kids get the sense that the world needs *them*. A lot of parents can't say no, and that completely screws up the kids. Then they have no boundaries. No limits, no structure. Nothing to rebel against. So they find something else to get their parents' attention. Instead of getting grounded for breaking a curfew they don't have, they end up on life support after OD'ing. I know it sounds dramatic, but it's not even the worst-case scenario.

I also know everybody loves their kids. I know that we want to be the cool parents, but a little common sense is nice, too. If your daughter is seventeen and the drinking age is twenty-one, you probably shouldn't let her go to that kegger or hip new nightclub. Nancy Reagan had it right, sorta. Just say no! It'll freak the kids out. They'll bitch about it to you, they'll bitch about it to their friends, and then they'll feel safe. Their world will have an order. I think I'm screwed up because my parents never said yes. Somewhere in the middle would have been nice.

Over my years of sobriety, I have had the opportunity to help others just as others helped me. Addiction is a tricky disease and most don't get it. But it is still disheartening when I, Mr. Sober Celebrity, cannot get through to my own kin. In the nineties my family was costing me a lot of money. So, with the help of my therapist, I set some limits. I will now pay for only one rehab, or lawyer's fee if there is a nonviolent crime, per family member.

This fund is also transferable to college if anyone ever makes it that far. I used to have most of my family on my payroll. Won't do that again. You can imagine the resentment when, because of cutbacks, I fired my stepmom. Although in her defense, no one since has put in the time, love, and energy she did answering my fan mail. I believe those three letters a week she had to respond to snowballed into the ocean of goodwill I receive to this day. She actually became pen pals with a bunch of these folks. Invited them to Iowa. To her home. She basically stalked them.

My sister Lori has been my biggest disappointment. After spending ten years in federal prison for drug dealing (she made her own crystal methamphetamine, so at least she wasn't supporting the Taliban) and missing out on raising her only child, she came back home with a new outlook. She was happy and grateful to be sober. She even said so in some newspaper articles (sounds familiar). I helped get her a job at the old meatpacking plant and she was on her way. Building self-esteem with every ham she defatted. And except for a little scam she helped her son, who operated the cash register at Kmart, engineer, she was toeing the line. After he was arrested and fired, she gave him the old "honesty is the best policy except when it comes to ratting out your big, bad mama" speech.

I secretly hoped that she'd drop me a little cash on payday. Nothing major, $25 or $30. Just something to put a little dent in the $250,000 she owed me. You know, good-faith money. But she didn't and that was OK with me as long as she stayed clean and sober. Then the reports started coming in: "Saw Lori drinking at the bar last night."

Lori wasn't supposed to be drinking; she wasn't even supposed to be in a bar. She was on parole, for God's sake. Called her up; she said that she was fine: "No meth, just a little beer." I smelled trouble, because I knew that no self-disrespecting drug addict would be satisfied with "just a little beer."

Then things happened fast. Lori quit her job at the plant. "What is she doing for money?" I asked my dad.

"Oh, she opened up an all-night antique shop, but they don't have many antiques."

Dad quickly scheduled an Arnold family portrait photo shoot.

This was something we'd done every ten years, and if we wanted to have all the kids together he had to act fast because the proverbial clock was tickin' (tweakin', actually).

On Memorial Day 2001, I drove in from a movie set in Chicago and they were all there. Sisters, brothers, stepsisters, stepbrothers, half brothers . . . you get the picture. Dad said that if I was going to get into it with anybody (i.e., ask about owed money) I had to please wait until "the picture takin' is over." So for Dad's sake I was extra nice, even shook the hand (what's left of it after an accident with a steel press on his first day of physical labor in ages) of my brother Scotty, who ironically seems to have a hard-on for me, which is weird because I'm the one that bought *him* a car.

The photographer, who said, "Smile," only once to my family, then, after seeing the discouraging results of his request, suggested a more introspective (mouths closed) look, was packing up. So, I took Lori outside for a mini-intervention. I told her that I loved her, but I knew she was doing drugs and if she was doing drugs I guaranteed she'd be selling them, if she wasn't already. I begged her to stop. Reminded her of the consequences. Even went so far as to tell her that I'd spoken to the sheriff (I had) and they were on her tail. She said that she appreciated my concern, but even though she had "experimented" with crystal recently she had it under control.

Four months later, I got the call. Lori had been busted again and was getting twelve years. Her new boyfriend, Matt (a lucky fella), was just an accomplice, so he would get only six. Lori and Matt got married in the Polk County lockdown, so in 2014 they can consummate their holey (yes, *holey*) union. She wrote me from jail and said she knows she screwed up again, but this time she "really gets it." That's nice. I wish her well. Her son will be nearly forty when she gets out. Maybe then they can finally spend some quality time together.

The Iowa streets are safer now, but the thing that pisses me off the most about Lori (besides the $250,000) is she was no dummy. She got all A's in school, at least until the eighth grade, when she got married, and it takes smarts to operate an interstate criminal enterprise. I'll bet she wishes she would've sold *Amway*.

I was at the 2002 Superbowl, going from one crazy-assed party to another. There was lots of booze and lots of drugs. Normal people were having a great time, but I was starting to get a little crabby when this dude that I vaguely recognized came up to me. I cringed, because I'm thinking it's another wasted talkaholic who loved me in *True Lies*, but he said, "Do you remember me?"

I hate that question. It instantly puts me on the spot. So I gave my standard, "Yeah, but remind me."

And he says, "I used to come to your house every week a few years ago when I was trying to get sober. I was struggling and couldn't even get a job as a production assistant and you told me not to worry about that, because my job was to stay sober and that if I did that everything else would fall into place. Well, this week I was named president of——Records" (a huge company)! Now I remembered him. "I just wanted to thank you, Tom." Cool, man. After I bragged to my fiancée Shelby I felt higher than everyone else combined at the New Orleans House of Blues Superbowl Bash. For every ten Loris there's one of these guys, and that's just enough to keep me going.

Every Tuesday night (Tuesdays with Arnie) my beautiful Beverly Hills home is invaded with drug addicts and alcoholics. Sober ones; they're the best kind. Some have been clean for twenty years and some twenty minutes. Some are famous, some infamous, and some are everyday people. All of us take a couple hours out of our hectic little lives to sit around, eat pizza, and listen to other people, strangers even, bitch and moan. And somehow this makes us all feel better about ourselves.

I usually dread my Tuesday night meeting. There's lots of good TV on Tuesday nights, but someone *always* says something that snaps some sense into me, that makes me feel grateful, even lucky. The talented and successful actors and writers and directors inspire me with their humility and humanity, but no more than the kid that gets up at four o'clock every morning to go pick strawberries.

Daddy, Were You Really a Movie Star?

Not to brag, babyface, but . . . kinda, sorta. And I wasn't the first member of my family to be in show business. My Uncle Bill made a documentary about Hitler, and my crazy Aunt Kay was in a Charmin toilet paper commercial. But, best of all, my cousin was married to the bass singer in the Gospel Gents. The Gospel Gents were a big-time Christian quartet from the lower Midwest. We were in awe of him until my grandma Dottie told us that during his Gospel travels Gospel cousin-in-law had picked up a second family. My cousin and her kids were crushed. Big scandal. No more Gents and, worst of all, Gospel Cous was my "in" to show business. Dammit!

When I worked at the meatpacking plant in Iowa I'd have this recurring dream that I was an actor in Hollywood and Robin Williams was my best friend. Then my alarm would go off at 5:15 A.M., I'd wake up in my crummy little apartment, look around, and realize I was dreaming and that I'd have to climb out of bed and into my cold-ass car and head to Hormel. I'd be so depressed that I willed myself to quit having this wonderful dream. It's just that it seemed so frickin' real.

Cut to 1994, I'm in San Francisco, my alarm goes off at 5:15

A.M., and I wake up and realize that I have to go to work because I'm making a movie with my new buddy, Mr. Robin Williams (5:15 A.M. still sucks). Of course, in real life we weren't best friends, but we did talk a lot (maybe it was the Chinese herbs we were taking to lose weight), and working with Robin and doing *Nine Months* was one of the best experiences of my career.

This was my first movie after *True Lies*, and if they'd all been this good I wouldn't be doing a basic cable sports show. The director was great, Chris Columbus (*Home Alone, Harry Potter and the Sorcerer's Stone, Mrs. Doubtfire*), and we had the best cast ever. Hugh Grant (*Four Weddings and a Funeral*), Julianne Moore (*The Shipping News, Hannibal*), Joan Cusack (*In and Out, Working Girl*), Jeff Goldblum (*The Big Chill, The Fly*), myself, and Robin (the nicest man alive). We worked hard, then hung out a little afterward. Usually at restaurants, but we were in San Francisco and if you're in San Francisco for five months you're eventually going to check out the Mitchell Brothers Emporium of Sex and Naked Girls and Stuff.

Technically, the establishment should've been called the Mitchell Brother, since one pornographer had killed the other, but the point is, besides the Golden Gate Bridge, Alcatraz, and that building that comes to a point, the Mitchell Brothers was San Francisco's most famous landmark. So of course, Hugh Grant and I checked it out. After I witnessed an intimate table dance where one lovely young lady injured another when she obviously went off script while performing the old foot-up-the-butt routine, I ran (literally) into Hugh, who'd also seen enough.

Perhaps because of him being from London and all Hugh had gotten himself all turned around, and ended up in a room with what he assumed was a peephole in the wall. During careful inspection while trying to make a visual, Hugh was nearly blinded when a very large black penis sprang forth from the next room. His wink reflex was the only thing that saved him from being officially "cockeyed."

Nine Months wrapped in January of 1995, and sadly we all headed our separate ways. But we would meet again in June in Los Angeles at the Four Seasons Hotel to promote the film. A press junket, as they are called, is when a hundred or so "journalists" are flown in from around the country to each spend three to five minutes asking actors the same three to five questions about their movie. It's a tedious but necessary exercise, and you have to make your own fun. This includes lying to writers, making up stories about the other actors, starting nasty rumors, and, if it's really boring, interrupting and heckling your costars during their interviews.

It's all fun and games unless something really stupid and newsworthy happens. So after Hugh interrupted me, I walked into his interview with *ABC* and asked him how it was going. He said, "Great, but not as great as last night when Tom was out with those hookers," to which I said, "Hugh's the one who picked up the hookers." Of course this exchange was all caught on camera.

Funny stuff until the next morning when I got a call from my publicist: "Did you hear about Hugh Grant?"

"Oh, my God, no. Is he dead?"

"Worse. Tom, he got arrested with a hooker."

"Wow," I said. "That's not so bad unless it was a man. . . . It wasn't a man, was it?" and she said, "Honestly, Tom, I'm looking at the picture and I can't tell."

That night on the news, *ABC* ran the clip of Hugh and me joking around about hookers. Smart move for a guy (me) who was getting married in a week. Good publicity for Chris Colombus's next big family film, too. *Fox*, the movie studio, was not pleased.

A lot of people asked me how a good-looking guy like Hugh

Grant, with a beautiful girlfriend like Elizabeth Hurley, could ever consider cruising for fifty-dollar hookers on a Sunday night in L.A. I guess a lot of people don't realize how boring L.A. is on Sunday nights. My opinion after spending plenty of time with Hugh and never seeing anything but a gentleman, to the point that I started thinking he might be a little light in the old loafers as it were, was that there must've been a combination of things to lead him astray:

1. Alcohol: Hugh had more than a little wine at dinner.
2. Loneliness: His girlfriend was on another continent.
3. Ignorance: Hugh told me later that if he'd even thought that his crime was actually a crime, he'd have been too scared to do it. I believe him; he was a wienie.

Hugh called the next day to apologize to me. "No need," I said. " 'Cause this goes a long way toward disproving the gay rumors I started at the press junket." [Ironically, Hugh and I were nominated for a MTV Movie Award for best kiss (see the movie its not what you think.)] He laughed. He told me that he was honestly relieved his date wasn't a man. He also told me that since he paid her in advance and the cops so rudely interrupted before dessert was served, he hoped for but did not count on a refund. But I could tell he was pretty scared, partly for his career—I mean, he did have this good guy Cary Grant sophisticated image—but I think he was mostly scared about damage to his relationship with the lovely Ms. Hurley. They'd had many years together and were obviously, above everything else, good friends. This is not the way any man wants a relationship to end.

Hugh and I talked a lot the next few days as he prepared to go on *Jay Leno*. I was booked on *Letterman* that same night. No doubt the least watched *Letterman* of all time. Dave introduced me by saying, "If I told you that Hugh Grant and Tom Arnold made a movie together and then I told you one of them was arrested with a prostitute, you'd figure it would be my next guest. Ladies and gentlemen, Tom Arnold." Dammit, man, Hugh was draggin' me down!

Leno was a success for Hugh, and now he was working feverishly trying to put his relationship back together. Apologies hadn't worked, so he went to Plan B: Get something bad on her so you can throw it back in her face and you can call it even. Then you can both start anew with a clean slate. Plan B might sound a little sick, but when you're humiliated and heartbroken you resort to drastic measures. I should know.

Hugh asked me if I'd heard any nasty Hollywood scoop on Elizabeth. I hadn't but said I'd ask around. A couple of calls later I had plenty of gossip and innuendo for my friend about the woman he loved. I told him I felt bad repeating what I had heard, that I didn't want him to suffer anymore. But as I spelled out the tale of a few years back of his gal and a wild party and a kitchen table and a spatula (I made that part up) Hugh actually seemed to be enjoying it. "Actually, I rather like it," he said.

"Please don't tell Elizabeth where you heard this," I said.

"I hope I won't have to, Tom," he replied.

Of course, he did have to reveal his source. I sensed that she never liked me (I really didn't know her that well) after that, and I also sensed that he was somehow banned from associating with me, too. Maybe he blamed the whole thing on me. I understand; I've taken a bullet for a friend or two before. But after Elizabeth took out a little more revenge on *Barbara Walters*, they did get back together for five years and that is what's important. I'm just glad that I could be of assistance.

I was really spoiled early on in my career. *Roseanne*, television's number-one show, was the first show I worked on. It was stocked with the best producers (Marcy Carsey, Tom Werner, Jay Daniel) and the finest actors (Rosey, John Goodman, Laurie Metcalf, Estelle Parsons) and writers (Rob Ulin, Bruce Helford, Chuck Lorre, Bob Myers, Amy Sherman, Eric Gilliand, Danny

Jacobson, Sid Youngers, Don Foster, Joel Madison, Mike Gandolfi, Betsy Bornes, Joss Whedon, Dave Raether, and many more) money could buy. We had a lot of turnover, some quit, unfortunately many more were fired, and it became my job to let some of the most talented and successful writer/producers in Hollywood know that they had to clean out their lockers. Funny thing was, most of them seemed relieved.

I started as a term writer and quickly progressed to staff writer, then producer, and finally executive producer. This meant that I could hire my friends. I've always had a soft spot for all forms of nepotism. But I didn't rest on my "fucking my way to the top" laurels. I actually learned how to become a decent writer. I also carved out my place on the show, working closely with the head writers on stories. Fortunately, I had built up a little trust with the star to the point where she didn't even know what the episodes were about until she read them each Monday morning. Unlike the first couple of years, when Roseanne had to micromanage every detail of her creation, this freed her up for her other passions, like psychotherapy and ballet. It also made me feel, rightly or not, that I was making a contribution to the show. I also realized what an honor it was to write for and watch Rosey, John Goodman, and Laurie Metcalf act on a daily basis.

A perfect example of my typically small but mighty contributions was the lesbian kiss episode with Mariel Hemingway. I'd asked Rosey what she thought about the possibility of her character locking lips with another woman (probably subconsciously hoping this might trigger real-life events), and she wasn't excited about the idea. I told her that we'd write a script and if she didn't like it, we'd throw it away (she used to do that a lot in the old days). But thankfully when she read it on that Monday, she liked it, and away we went. She also liked the script I wrote about PMS based on our life and *Apocalypse Now*.

ABC didn't like the lesbo smooch and only agreed to run the episode if the kiss was unseen. But since I felt we were protecting Rosey's character as we always did (Mariel initiated the kiss and Roseanne responded by wiping her "soiled" lips on her shirt), I insisted that we turn over our version of the show and *ABC* could choose to air it or not. As word got out, there were complaints that this kiss would be bad for America. Now *I* was offended. I don't want to live in a country where two adult women cannot make out. Especially if one of them is hot.

Finally, the day before its scheduled airing, the network came to their senses (knees) and lots of viewers tuned in and turned on, baby! I watched the kiss at a big gay party thrown by the big gay writers Stan Zimmerman and Jim Berg. When the climatic moment came midway through the show, the room erupted with flamboyant jubilation. Tears even. Personally, I didn't think it was that big a deal, but I reacted the exact same way a few years later when I watched my buddy David Wells pitch a perfect game for the New York Yankees.

When we weren't creating magic, Roseanne and I usually got along pretty well on the set. Probably a lot like Lucy and Desi, only with more biting, pinching, wrestling, and cookies. The fact that Rosey and I wore the same size pants was not the only thing we had in common. Abandonment issues were evident when I signed my first solo deal for my very own HBO Special, *Tom Arnold: The Naked Truth*.

Although I loved and appreciated Roseanne's coattail opportunities, this would be my chance to shine, on my own, just by myself, if of course she agreed to coproduce and appear in it. I ended up doing three *Naked Truths* and I had a pretty impressive roster of support: Jim Carrey, Adam Sandler, Chris Farley, Ben Stiller, Rob Schneider, Frank Zappa, Martin Mull, Fred Willard, and Laurie Metcalf all pitched in.

Judd Apatow (*Freaks and Geeks*, *The Cable Guy*) was the head writer, and Peter Segal (*Anger Management*, *Tommy Boy*) directed. The specials, dealing with fame, relationships, and the survival of the planet, turned out pretty darn well, and people seemed to like them. Thank God for low expectations! We even got nominated for some *Cable Ace Awards*.

But the road to success was a bumpy one and began the first day. Since we were shooting on a budget and obtaining shooting permits in Beverly Hills was a costly endeavor, we were using Judd's grandmother's lovely home as our first location. Imagine my excitement. My dream of doing something completely on my own, with the help of some of the most talented people in Hollywood, was coming true. Roseanne and I were getting makeup administered when, caught up in a moment, I made a positive comment about the well-toned physicality of my hairstylist.

This innocent compliment did not sit too well with the little woman, and before I knew it a large hand was embedded into the side of my chubby face. The good side of my chubby face. Realizing that I was no longer camera-ready and, more important, that my costar, coproducer, and cospouse was exiting stage left, I followed her to her car with a mix of apologizing-begging-demanding that she stay.

The fact was that if she left, the shoot was over, the special was over, and so were any fantasies I'd had of potentially standing on my own professionally. There was a loud and vulgar discussion on Judd's grandma's well-manicured front lawn. The assistant director, a six-four, 290-pound behemoth named, appropriately, Oak, tried to intercede before the authorities were called and we were shut down for legal purposes. Big old Oak was frightened. I remember the panic I felt and the look of fear on the crew's faces, which was in sharp contrast to the look of shock I'd seen on other people's faces whenever Roseanne told them that they had to hire me.

The crew were helpless, scared children and Roseanne and I were the selfish feuding parents. Finally, after much groveling and perhaps a couple of man tears, as a Hail Mary I threw in something about getting some Ben & Jerry's and starting from square one and I saw that click in her eyes and knew she was back with us and that things would be OK. Until the next time. The rest of the shoot went well that day and nobody complained about the handprint bruise on my right cheek or the New York Super Fudge Chunk stains on Rosey's summer dress.

Talk about nowhere to go but down. My first movie costarring role was in *True Lies* and my first real scene in a film ever was with Academy Award–winning actor Dustin Hoffman in *Hero*. Stephen Frears, the great and gentle British director (*Dangerous Liaisons, High Fidelity*), cast me as Bernie the bartender, but I had to meet Dustin first. I was nervous as hell to meet and try to impress one of my idols. Would he be a snob (couldn't blame him)? Would he be crabby, aloof, mean? But Dustin was a pleasant surprise.

After I rousted him from a ferocious game of tackle football he was quarterbacking with a group of homeless men in an abandoned lot, Dustin joined me in his trailer. He seemed funny, self-effacing, and a little ornery, but in a good way. He just wanted to talk, so I regaled one of the world's four or five finest actors with my tales from the meatpacking plant. Tales he later recited while promoting *Hero* on *Larry King.* I was incredibly embarrassed that this acting god was constantly being asked about what Tom Arnold was really like.

The filming went smoothly except for the director's massive heart attack. He occasionally had a hard time keeping track of his star. That and lots of bangers and mash led to Stephen's cardiovascular discomfort. During my close-ups (I only had five scenes, but they were all with Dustin) I'd do my lines and Mr. Hoffman would respond in Chinese. Just to keep me on my toes.

After the movie wrapped, I was back in Iowa and I got a call on my cell phone. It was Dustin saying that he'd seen the movie and that he thought I was very good in it. This was too much for my heart to take, too good, too unbelievable, so I hung up on him before I died. Clint Eastwood once walked up to my stepmother and told her, unsolicited, that I was a good actor. I'm glad I wasn't there; that most definitely would've killed me.

Hero came out and did so-so, but I loved the film and highly recommend it. I happened to be in a theater with my then-wife and then-stepkids when a trailer for *Hero* appeared. My big ugly mug was all over it, right next to Dustin's. I don't think I've ever had a prouder professional moment. The stepkids even seemed impressed. I've gotten to know Dustin and his very nice and normal family a little these last few years. We're not buddies or anything, but he sat on my lap a few times (of course, I've got the pictures to prove this) when I played Santa over the holidays in Maui.

In 1992, I got my first and favorite network television series. *The Jackie Thomas Show* still holds up today. It was a combination of *Buffalo Bill*, the groundbreaking Dabney Coleman vehicle, and the not-yet-produced *Larry Sanders Show*. I played an insecure, tyrannical, not-so-smart sitcom star from Iowa, and surprisingly, I never got nominated for an acting *Emmy*. We had the best time slot in television, Tuesday nights right after *Roseanne*.

The first-week ratings came out and the wife was number one and we were number two. Sweet. But that wouldn't last and every Wednesday morning we'd get the ratings fax and cringe as my show's numbers dropped. Looking back, and at the risk of sounding unappreciative, *Roseanne* was probably not the best lead-in for us, since we had a male-dominated audience. At the end of the season *ABC* came to us and said that they'd bring the show back next year if we changed it completely. I would no longer be a TV star from Iowa playing a butcher, but instead I'd be an Iowa butcher with some cute little kids. I didn't see how Jackie Thomas, the Jackie Thomas that we created, could ever be a good parent, or a good butcher for that matter. So we passed. The headline on the front page (not the entertainment page but the frickin' front page) of the next day's *USA Today* blurted: "*ABC* Cancels Tom Arnold!" *Fox* offered to take the show, but we were stupid and didn't accept. We figured that *Fox* was a fledgling network and who knew if they'd be around for very long. We figured wrong.

The week *Jackie Thomas* premiered I was booked to host *Saturday Night Live*. By myself. I'd done the show a couple of times with Rosey, but this was all me. So when Rosey showed up at my hotel to surprise me I was a complete selfish, unappreciative jerk. After all she'd done for me, I was afraid that her presence could take away some of my "glory." Of course this hurt her feelings. Of course she wanted to leave. But I couldn't let her go. I blocked the door and basically held her hostage until she wore down and accepted my apology. Goddammit, that still makes me cringe. Not my finest moment.

After *Jackie Thomas's* one-season run, I moved to *CBS* and *Tom* (an original title). I should've waited a season and regrouped, but my pride and ego prompted me to rush and get another show on the air. I enjoyed *Tom*. A bunch of the *Jackie Thomas* crew came with me, including Alison Laplaca and Steve Pepoon. The show was about a farmer, his wife, and their five kids trying to get by and build their dream home. *Tom* was canceled in 1994.

After that, I did a bunch of movies. Some worked; most didn't. But even the ones that bombed (*The Stupids, Carpool, Big Bully, McHale's Navy*) were usually good experiences. I had fun, was paid very well, and got to work with some directors (John Landis and Arthur Hiller) who'd made some of my favorite movies ever (*Animal House* and *Trading Places* and *The Inlaws* and *The Out of Towners*). Looking back, I should've slowed down, been more selective, but each offer was better than the last and as a guy like me is still shocked when I get any offer to act in any movie, I thought I'd better take them all because each offer might actually be my last. I almost made that happen.

I've learned that you've got to pace yourself. You've got to be able to say no. I've also learned that, at least for the time being, I'm a much better supporting actor than movie star. I've gotten more props for the one day I worked on *Austin Powers* than the two and a half years I spent starring in movies before that. I don't want to brag (but I will). I brought "How about a *courtesy flush*" into the American lexicon. With my luck, "Don't blow out your O ring" will be on my tombstone.

In 1997 I signed with the *WB* for another sitcom. I was rapidly running out of networks. *The Tom Show* (another bad title) was about a single father of two daughters, who moved back home to St. Paul to start his career over at a public-access TV station after being fired by his ex-wife, an Oprah-like talk show host, who, in a dream come true, was played by Kiss's Gene Simmons's main squeeze, the beautiful Playmate Shannon Tweed (whose centerfold adorned my college dorm room and helped me get to sleep on a lot of cold lonely Iowa nights). The great Ed McMahon played my boss, and Michael Rosenbaum (*Smallville*, and one of People magazines 50 most-eligibile bachelors) played my assistant. We really had a good time and I was disappointed that we didn't (per usual) make it to a second year.

You know you've been in this business awhile when actors who played your kids grow up. Andy Lawrence (brother of Joey and Matt) was four when he played my youngest son on *Tom*. He was too young to read, so he memorized all of his lines, and mine. When I screwed up, which was often, he would correct me. His mom, Donna, was horrified, but I loved it. The Lawrences are one of those rare show-biz-type families who did it right. They are as loving and sweet as any family I've ever met. I'd say that they were normal, but normal's not so good anymore. Andy, who's fourteen as I write this, is no longer a chubby young kid but a handsome muscle-bound young stud who would be one of the groomsmen in my wedding to Shelby. Now as far as the girls who played my daughters, there's nothing more disconcerting than getting your hopes up while being approached in a bar by a hot babe and hearing the words: "Remember me?" Then:

"No, but I'd like to."

"You played my dad in . . ."

"Oh, shit! That's right. I've still got the ashtray you made me at sleep-away camp." Am I sad or what?

Daddy, I Bet You Was Always
Nice to Everybody

Well, not always, darlin', but I learned my lesson. It's important to be kind. I always tell my wife, Shelby, that if she's going to be cruel to me, do it in the form of a joke. That helps ease the sting. But it still has to be funny. During my trials and tribulations, I've heard many a joke about myself. Carson (Johnny, not Daly), Arsenio, Letterman, Leno, they've all had their fun, and the funny jokes never bothered me, even though sometimes they hit a little close to home (I have a book on my shelf that David Letterman held up after Roseanne dumped me: *Boy, Am I Screwed*, by Tom Arnold). Jay Leno even calls to ask if it's OK if he makes fun of me. He's nice.

Chris Farley phoned me in a panic once when Roseanne was hosting *Saturday Night Live* and said that she wanted him to play me and that she was going to slam me good. He was nervous because he didn't want to offend his old buddy Tom. Again, I said, "Do it, but be funny." It probably would've been funny if Chris wasn't so damn nervous. If you're going to satirize an American institution, you can't do it halfway or it just doesn't work.

After a few years of seeing other comedians use me as a

punch line, I had a revelation: hell, man, I could do that. So now my comedy is based on the theory that if something about me is embarrassing (divorce, movie bombing, TV show cancellation, weight gain, penis size), I'm going to talk about it before anyone else gets the chance. That way I get the laughs at my own expense.

There's also an unwritten rule that you can only make fun of people bigger than yourself. Back in the days when George Bush Sr. was president, Roseanne and I used to take our shots at the man, especially after he stated publicly that Roseanne's performance of the national anthem was "disgraceful"; how rude (although the awesome Barbara Bush defended Rosey, calling her a "brave lady"). A couple of years later, Maria Shriver invited me to dinner with her and Arnold and the Bushes. I told her that I'd love to join them and laughingly mentioned that I was glad George Sr. never heard the jokes (not all funny) I'd made about him on TV: "Actually, Tom, he has heard them."

The next day, I sent George a note. I apologized for some of my comments (the not-funny ones) and said that he deserved more respect than that. Literally three days later (I have no idea how this happened so quickly; maybe the CIA was involved) I received a handwritten letter from the former president saying, basically, that he understood and of course he and Barbara had no hard feelings and, in fact, he'd heard I was quite a nice guy. Something like that's enough to make you love the man's whole family.

The first time I can ever remember feeling compassion was on the playground at the Anne G. Wilson Elementary School. There was a girl, sorta plain-looking and chubby, who just stood and watched the other kids play. While most seemed to ignore her, she always caught my eye, and finally one day I asked her if she would join us in a game of coop (a team game where us boys chased one another around and, when caught, were dragged, kicking and screaming, back to the imaginary chicken coop, where we remained until being freed with a slap on the hand by a teammate).

My buddies were horrified: "No girls can play coop, Tom!" But I felt for her. Why? Maybe because I was a good kid with a big heart, or maybe because I was foreseeing the sort of women I'd be with in the future. But I was not always so kind as a kid, and it came back to haunt me at my ten-year high school reunion. An attractive woman (Sue H.) walked up to me and shouted, "Remember in junior high when you and your friends used to call me Sweat Hog? Well, now I'm hot and you're fatter than I ever was!" So true. I asked if we could perhaps continue this discussion in private over a cocktail and she laughed in my big, fat face.

The bigger reason that I want my children to be kind is because by the time you realize the error of your ways and want to make amends, it might be too late. Elaine M. was in my third-grade class. She was not unusual other than she had older parents and she dressed better and was smarter than the rest of us. But we constantly made fun of her. We tormented her. I can remember chasing her around school and calling her names. I remember her sweaty, panicked face, that she was breathless and truly frightened, and I remember that we all laughed. Then we did it again the next day. This went on for a year. What the hell was wrong with me? As much pain and humiliation as I'd felt from the big kids at school, the punches, the kicks, the de-pantsings, the poison ivy rubbed in my face, you'd think I would've known better. You'd think.

Many years later, when I got sober, I wrote an inventory of my life and the persons that I'd harmed and I tried to make amends to them all. I gave Tim Allen back the money I'd stolen from him when I cashed a bunch of his fifteen-dollar Improv Comedy Club checks in the late eighties. Our names were right next to each other in the file, and the cashier was always a little tipsy. I sent $1,000 to the McDonald's in Iowa City where I worked in college (I gave away a lot of free food). This amends went well and when I apologized, the owner almost choked up.

But I did forget to mention the box with 6,000 Big Game pull tabs I heisted. My roommates and I sat up all night and pulled and pulled until our sticky fingers bled. By dawn's early light we had still not won the $1 million grand prize. But we had won 300 Big Breakfasts and 200 Hot Cakes and Sausage. So after the next day's all-night party, me and my buddy Mo headed to Mickey D's to pick up our complimentary breakfast for 500.

I parked behind the Dumpster and ducked down in my car because: (1) I didn't want to be recognized, because employees were not eligible to play the Big Game, especially if they stole the prizes; and (2) I didn't want to be recognized because I was supposed to be at work. When Mo got to the counter he encountered some resistance. The Big Game was still on and he would be able to cash in his tickets, but if he'd read the extra-fine print, he would've known that you could only cash in one item at a time.

Boy, there's gonna be some disappointed drunks at Tom's house, Mo thought. But he said, "Boy, there's gonna be some disappointed kids back at the Children's Hospital." And they fell for it. They even pitched in and assisted Mo in loading up the car. The man in the driver's seat with the stocking cap pulled over his face was no help at all.

I also sent $3,500 to Paul's Discount Department Store, another former place of employment. Every night I'd leave work with my new gym bag. Only I didn't bring a gym bag to work and it definitely wasn't full of brand-new sporting goods.

As I worked through my long list (ex-girlfriends, the Student Loan Association) I thought about Elaine M. and I felt worse about harassing her than any heinous thing I'd ever done (including the Tim Allen caper). I wanted to look her up and apologize. I would tell her that it was not her fault, that I was a jerk, and that I was very, very sorry for my behavior. I figured that she'd accept my apology, as most others had, if for no other reason than because I was this big celebrity and she would have a nice story to tell her kids.

But before I could unburden my soul, I found out some very bad news. Elaine had died in a tragic accident. There would be no "I accept your apology" hug for me. I would just have to live with my deserved guilt. The best I could do now was say a prayer for her and for me and pass this lesson on to my own children. It's been twelve years since I tried to make things right with Elaine M. and there are still nights when it takes me a little longer to get to sleep than it would've if I'd always been kind.

Daddy, I Bet Everybody Was Nice to You When You Were a Little Kid

Almost everybody, munchkin (family doesn't count). Experts say that at least 20 percent of Americans have been sexually abused as children. I'm guessing that's about 99 percent for celebrities. Not just because they all talk about it, sing about it, write about it, but because the effects of this abuse make for some pretty serious celebrity potential. The bottomless need for love of all kinds from anybody, everybody. All the time. The addictive, inappropriate behavior that pays so well and the need to commingle with the same. Celebrities are freaks, aliens, monsters, and gods. They are the most insecure people in the world, with the biggest egos on the planet. Great combo. And fame just guarantees that the hard candy outside the package gets stroked but does nothing to take care of the soft, gooey middle.

I doubt all celebrities were born that way. They can be cured and humbled, but why would they? As Jim Belushi once said to me during one of my brief periods of singlehood, "Celebrity is a Gold Card for pussy; enjoy yourself, Tom." James Woods offered a pearl of wisdom that same night. "Tom, stay away from bimbos . . . for a little while anyway." That's solid advice from a guy that's dated a nineteen-year-old underwear model or two. I like pussy, but I also like a little serenity. So I needed to get centered.

Ironically, the story starts on Center Street back in my old Ottumwa, Iowa, neighborhood. Dad worked hard and Mom liked to party hardy. So since I was only four, Lori three, and Scotty one, we needed some quality adult supervision. After what appeared to be a pretty lax screening process, our sixteen-year-old neighbor (I'll call the asshole Larry) was selected. Larry was very attentive, especially to Little Tommy. And we played lots and lots of games. Unfortunately, they all involved our penises.

I never told anybody. What would I tell them? Dad and I never had "the pervert talk." I didn't know what the hell was going on anyway. It just seemed silly, but Larry enjoyed it, so what the heck.

After my parents broke up, we got a real (non-predatory pedophile) baby-sitter. Now poor Larry had to lure me all the way across the street to his house. It ended after a couple years. I don't remember why it ended; I guess eventually we just drifted apart.

Cut to twenty-five years later. I'm in rehab and the nosy doctors are trying to figure out why I'm so fucked up. They asked me if I'd ever been molested, and I said yes. (Actually, I said yes to all their questions.) I'd never talked about it before. It didn't seem like good party conversation, which is surprising, because when you do as much coke as I did, you pretty much cover everything, every night. But now it was time to speak up. To bury my demons. To unburden my soul. So I shared the most intimate and humiliating story of my life with twelve of the most fucked up strangers I'd never met, my detox support group.

They listened; they cried; they nodded off. But my secret was no more and I was free. Time to go on *Sally Jesse Raphael* and tell America. Roseanne told me that my tale triggered memories of her own, and away we went.

After doing *A Very Special Geraldo*, I stopped in Iowa to

proudly attend my sister Lori's most recent prison sentence hearing. A nice crowd had gathered at the Des Moines Federal Courthouse. As a big-time small-town drug dealer she had accumulated a sizable following. Suddenly the judge called a break in the proceedings to figure out where the annoying sounds were coming from (my brother Mark was making fart noises with his sweaty hands). One of the unwashed masses walked up and said that she saw me on *Sally* and even though I didn't mention Larry by name, this sweet little gal knew exactly who I was talking about. She was married to Larry's younger brother, and, according to her, he had a tale to tell himself. I don't know why Larry even bothered to leave his house. Sounds like he was getting all he could handle at home. She also told me that Larry was now a successful businessman and church leader living right here in River City, and he had adopted several boys. Now I had to get involved, but I needed a game plan. One that would not end with me and my sister as cellmates.

After looking up a bunch of other former kids from the old neighborhood and talking to my therapist in L.A., I decided on a confrontation. But it would take some serious planning. I hired a private eye who tracked the creep down and located his place of business. This was where I would make my play. No sense confronting him at his home. That would scare his kids, and I figured they'd been through enough. I practiced for a couple of weeks on my shrink so I would be able to remain calm yet get my message across. Finally, he said I was ready! "That's perfect, Tom; only do it without the choking."

On Monday morning I flew to Des Moines International (seriously?) Airport, hopped in a limo, met the PI, and was off to the showdown. He led me to the local and asked if I wanted some company. I told him to sit tight, but if he heard gunshots being fired it was probably trouble, since I was unarmed. He showed me that he was packin' and assured me that if it got ugly he'd get involved and I wouldn't die alone. Super!

As I entered the building I wondered if I'd recognize Larry. I hadn't seen him in many years, and if there was a misidentification on my part it would be, at the very least, embarrassing. I walked up to the receptionist! "Hi, I'm here to see Larry."

Remember, even then I was famous, at least in Iowa, and she was surprised: "Oh, my God, what are you doing here?"

"I just stopped in to see an old friend." I was so calm.

She picked up the phone to call him and I said, "Please don't do that; it'll ruin the surprise!"

She agreed and my timing for once was perfect. As he walked out of his office to lunch, I met him in the hall. When he saw me, he turned white. He knew. "Hey, what . . . are . . . you . . . doing . . . here?"

I was stunned. He looked exactly the same, just older. But I buckled down: "I'm here to give you back the pain and shame you caused me as a child, and if you tried to do those things to me now I'd break your fuckin' neck."

Without missing a beat he said, "Your memories are wrong!" Sounded like he'd been down this road before.

Then he stuck his thick finger in my chest and I froze. I was scared. I remembered the power he'd had over me as a kid. I remembered the room behind the porch at his parents' house. I remembered the way it looked. I remembered the way it smelled. Then I remembered that I was a six-two, 250-pound thirty-year-old man with anger management issues and I grabbed his finger and bent it inward (I milked his mouse; thanks, Ruth!) and I said, "Touch me again and I'll kick your fucking teeth out in front of your employees."

Word of a celebrity in the house had spread and a nice crowd had gathered. Now Larry looked frightened, but my work here was complete. "Keep him away from your kids," I yelled to all as I left, "and watch my new HBO Special!"

I strolled outside and sucked in the cold Iowa air. I felt great! Called Rosey and reported my drama. She was excited, too, so

I headed back to L.A. to spread the news. I'd done it. It was over. All behind me now. I was cured. Then a week later I got a call. The PI had done a little more digging, and old Larry was about to adopt another boy. Gosh, I never thought of that. Remember, the average molester exploits 100 victims, and this lazy deviant was probably raising his own. These bastards cannot be stopped; you can only hope to contain them.

So I was off to Iowa again to meet with the governor and his staff. I was told that there was nothing they could do, statute of limitations and all, but they would look into it. Wink, wink. Soon after, I got a call. The adoption had been denied. Wow, not only was I healed, but maybe I actually had helped somebody else! Now I'd really done everything humanly possible and I could get on with my life! Just one more thing. I had a couple of my farmhands print up 100 posters listing the perv's name, address, and crimes and then put them up late one night on every telephone pole, bus stop, and park bench in a six-block radius of Larry's house. A little heads-up from Big Tom to the Little Tommys in the vicinity.

Daddy, Did You Ever Save Anybody's Life Like Spider-Man Does?

Yes, of course, cupcake, and not just *anybody's* life, either. Daddy doesn't like to brag, but in 1991 I was reading the special Christmas issue of the *Star* tabloid and I learned that Peter Criss, original drummer for Kiss, was a homeless alki living under a pier in Santa Monica. So I immediately jumped in my Bentley turbo and headed west. If you know sunny Santa Monica, you know it's like a homeless Woodstock, and for good reason: warm, comfortable climate and plenty of outdoor cafés stocked with generous liberals who rarely eat all their food. My mission was to find the man who sang "Beth," an important song from my youth (I had a girlfriend named Beth and we used to make out on the golf course), and get him sober and then back into show business where he belonged.

Simple enough, but I needed a little luck, since my loving wife and stepkids expected me home in forty-five minutes for our big Jewish Christmas dinner. The clock was ticking, but lightning struck as I pulled up to the first group of homeless I saw milling around: "Hey, I'm Tom Arnold. Have you seen Peter Criss, the down-on-his-luck former drummer from Kiss?"

"Why, yes," said a crusty surfer type who I estimated was

somewhere between fifteen and fifty-five years old. "Follow me, dude," he said.

I met one of my childhood heroes at the sleaziest motel on Ocean Avenue. The *Star* had given Peter temporary accommodations so that they could keep an eye on him for future heart-warming articles. Much like the rock star of old, Peter had many friends (fifteen or so were in his tiny stanky-smelling room). Although I'd never met him, the years had not been kind, and he did not have his "cat" makeup on. But one look at that thick rock star hair and I knew I'd met my man. "Hi, I'm Tom Arnold and I'm going to help you." He seemed confused, so I pulled him outside to talk away from the entourage, crack smoke, and vomit.

"Peter, I've got to run home, take a hot shower, and spend a few hours with my family . . . but I'll be back at seven and I can save your life then," I said.

"Sounds good, man," he said. "Bring more whiskey."

After some glorious holiday family psychodrama, I made a few calls and loaded up a couple of sober buddies, Dallas and Bob, and headed back to the party. We would bring Peter to a 12-Step meeting tonight, then check him into rehab tomorrow. I always dreamed of being in the real lifesaving business, but I had no idea that it would be this easy. Turns out it's not.

Upon my arrival at the motel, the night clerk (do they have to look like child molesters?) informed me that Peter and company had been evicted. Panic set in; what if I couldn't find him? This could severely fuck with my newfound "hero" status. So we hit the streets. This was L.A., so celebrity worship was just as important a part of the culture as public social responsibility and bulimia. Even homeless-celebrity worship. So we simply followed Peter's "buzz"—"he peed here," "he passed out there"— until we discovered him on the beach signing autographs and accepting gifts of beer and pot from adoring fans. The tabloids had once again called a kind and enabling nation into action.

We dragged him into my car and headed for a fancy rock 'n' roll alcoholic meeting in Hollywood. Heroing can be a nasty business, and my first taste of that came as we drove off and I realized that my new buddy smelled like a combination of rotting hay and horseshit. I used to work on a farm. Happy childhood memories aside, it was windows down and 100 mph to Sunset Boulevard.

The meeting was great and Peter got some much-needed beauty rest. After a more leisurely drive back to the beach, at which time I resolved to burn my clothes and car, I checked my sponsee into the finest forty-five-dollar motel in So Cal. Peter suggested the Four Seasons and I smiled because I knew that at least his ego was in recovery. I told him to stay put, absolutely no parties, and I'd take him to the hospital the next night, when a bed was opening up.

That night, as I was exfoliating myself with a wire brush in the pool house shower I'd been banished to, I felt good. The next morning, I called to check on Peter and he told me that he was going to Boston to live with his old girlfriend. She'd found him through the *Star*. I called her and begged her to let him stay in L.A. and go to rehab. His life depended on it, and so does this story. Although she hadn't seen him in ten years, she said she still loved him and she could really help him, but she promised to let him stay in L.A.

That evening I went to Peter's room and was informed by the gang (I had told him *absolutely no parties!*) that he had been picked up by a limo and whisked off to the airport. I was pissed. But why was I pissed? Was it because I cared about his well-being or was it because I wanted to brag about my lifesaving heroics to my future children? I decided that maybe his old girlfriend could help him, even more than me, and just the fact that I tried counts for something in God's eyes. So I kicked all the smelly bastards out of the room, closed up shop, and went home.

Later that night, I received a frantic phone call from Peter's girlfriend. He had finally arrived in Boston after being kicked off the plane in Chicago. He was safely at her home, but there were two problems: (1) he was throwing up everywhere, and (2) he wasn't Peter Criss. Problem number one could be solved temporarily by giving him some beer, but number two was your fault, bitch, "I begged you not to fly him out there!"

I felt a little embarrassed that I'd been suckered by this impostor and even more embarrassed that I'd learned the "facts" of this case from the *Star*. But I realized that now this poor nobody fucker really needed somebody's help. He was in Boston, so I got ahold of some guys (the only people I knew in Boston) that had a lot more experience in the hero department: Aerosmith (Steven Tyler, Joe Perry, et al). They picked him up and got him some help out there. He was having one weird day.

I don't know what happened to the impostor after treatment, but I did get to meet the real, nonalcoholic Peter Criss and "the girlfriend" on *Donahue*. According to the real Criss, they'd never even met, and a couple months later I read in *USA Today* that she was claiming to be Billy Idol's girlfriend. I called and gave Billy a heads-up. I like to help. I also gave a deposition in the real Peter Criss's lawsuit against the *Star*. Gene Simmons heard about this story and called Peter, and soon after Peter put back on the cat suit and rejoined Kiss for a huge sold-out world tour. For a brief moment I actually felt Hanks-like. I am the man!

Daddy, Will My Penis Be Big Like Yours When I Grow Up?

Bigger, Son, if there is a God. The guy who said there is no such thing as bad press never had an ex-wife who said he has a three-inch penis on *Saturday Night Live*. But like I say, even a 747 looks small if it lands in the Grand Canyon.

My penis is fine. My present beloved even says it's big-"ish." Maybe because I undersell it. If someone expects petite and gets medium, they're impressed. "Wow, did you supersize this thing?" The truth is not so funny. According to the tape measure that sits permanently on my nightstand, my wiener, at game time, is actually, ever so slightly, above average (especially when I press down the surrounding fat pocket). But I think all men wish theirs were a little bigger. Dieting helps; the thinner you are the bigger it looks (Tommy Lee). Shaving works a little, too (Tommy Lee). Did you know that the penis is the only part of the human body that doesn't gain or lose weight? God made it that way; otherwise the world would be full of 800-pound guys.

Dad, Mommy Says She Prays to the Good Lord Every Night That When I Grow Up, I Have Her Body and Not Yours

See there; your mommy really loves you, pumpkin. When I was ten I hit 100 pounds and I felt too fat to take off my shirt. At twenty I was 200 pounds and I said, "That's it; I'm getting this weight thing under control." When I hit 300 at thirty I sensed a pattern. Some of my Iowa buddies thought I should go for it. So we looked up the record in *Guinness*: 1,450 pounds. I was "only" gaining 10 pounds a year and I didn't think I would live to be 145 (146 if I really wanted to own the record). So once again I decided to do something drastic. Normal diet and exercise was never an option for me, but I'd seen the incredible results Oprah had achieved using *Optifast*. She'd lost like sixty-seven pounds by just drinking these chocolate shakes for a few months. Oprah resembled E.T. now and she looked like she could keel over at any moment because her small body could no longer support her huge head. But I knew that this was the plan for me. So for sixty-five days I ate no food, only three shakes a day. I lost about 100 pounds and my mind. I have a hunch that Oprah did not supplement her shakes with mounds of cocaine, but the results were the same. I was fearful that any day now my massive skull would telescope into my weakened minibody. But all good things come to an end. I remember one day thinking it was a little unusual that I hadn't gone to the bathroom properly for three weeks. But I was getting so many compliments that I shrugged it off.

This was about the time that Roseanne and I went from being friends to being a little more than friends. One of our first dates was to a high school prom. Neither of us had gone to ours. She got pregnant and didn't finish high school, and my girlfriend Ann dumped me two days before mine. Ann was sweet. She said that although she didn't like me anymore, she and her new boyfriend thought it would be OK if we still went. "No thanks," I said. Yeah, when I was young I still had a little pride. So Rosey (thirty-seven) and I (thirty) made some calls and showed up at some high school in the San Fernando Valley all dressed up and ready to rock. I heard we were a big hit. It felt good to be a role model! I don't remember much about the night because I was so high and hungry. I just kept thinking, *God, don't let me die here.* I used to think that a lot.

The next day I was at my apartment in the middle of a meeting with a cute eighteen-year-old girl, whose Palm Beach parents had hired me to write her a comedy act. Suddenly I felt some major cramps. I started sweating profusely, which wasn't that unusual, but this time I knew something was wrong. I excused myself to the rest room, remembering that I hadn't taken a dump in about a month. I was doubled over in pain, but nothing was working. *God, please don't let me die here,* I thought once again. In an act of desperation that probably saved my life, I reached into a drawer and pulled out a long darning needle. I have no idea how it got there, but the Lord does work in mysterious ways. The disgusting thing inside of me was huge and round and solid as a rock. So I feverishly (literally) went to work with the needle, breaking up this brick and relieving my pain. After a quick shower to wash away, among other things, three quarts of blood, I was as good as new and I was then ready to meet the

114

new challenge of explaining my forty-five-minute absence to a sweet, innocent little rich girl: "I always take a shower during all my comedy meetings; it makes me funnier." She understood. So we worked a little, made out; then she jumped into her new Corvette and drove out of Van Nuys, back to Beverly Hills, never to be seen again.

Daddy, Why Were You Married to That Crabby Lady from TV before Mommy?

Well, gorgeous, for one thing, when "Crabby Lady" and I got together, Mommy was only sixteen. Plus, the better question might be: "Why did Crabby TV Lady marry Daddy?" You have to remember that when Roseanne and I got married she was the biggest star in America (yes, at the time, even bigger than Cruise, Hanks, or Clancy). She had the number-one TV show. Her book was number one. She played huge concerts and was starring in a movie with Miss Meryl Streep. My biggest accomplishment was the thirty-day chip I'd gotten at the New Beginnings rehab center. We were America's worst nightmare: white trash with money. Still, people often ask me, Why? Why Roseanne? Well, like myself, "the Domestic Goddess" was not the perfect physical specimen. Although when you're in love you overlook things. Today I have a hard time watching the reruns on TV. Who were these people? They are huge! But it was easy to love her then because she has a genius that's intoxicating. She also makes you feel that you might have some of that magic, too. I remember the tingling in my spine the first time I watched her read one of my scripts. (At first, I thought it was a little stroke; actually, it might have been.) Plus, for the first time in my life I didn't feel fat, ever. Naked, even. Perfectly toned women are too much pressure. But if she's got a little cellulite she sure as hell can't bitch about your love handles. I'll take a big chick who finds me really attractive over a skinny one who doesn't any day. Although my goal these last few years has been to find a medium one who finds me moderately sexy. Rosey and I started off well, but we are living proof that marriage can ruin a good friendship.

Rosey and I played a lot, but we also fought a lot. She was dangerous. She has a low center of gravity and she'd get a running start on you. She's not a very big woman, despite what people think, and she's very agile. She has excellent lateral movement. Plus, she was so good at throwing things. Expensive things. Hard things. Roseanne did not like to be ignored. Our fights were not always private, either. We had a nice row at Bob Hope's ninetieth birthday party.

We had just performed a little loving husband and adoring wife comedy skit that was amusing only to us and Bob's cue card guy (the busiest man in show business). Everything was going well, but as we were leaving, Rosey got into a small altercation with a security guard. She wanted his Bob Hope's ninetieth-birthday button. I felt sorry for the guy because I'm sure this button would go in his home collection of cool Hollywood stuff. He probably has a little grotto set up in the corner of the living room. And I'm sure his wife bitches about it every day. But Rosey wanted that button and he finally said she could have it. I stuck my big nose in there and said, "Honey, that's not very nice; give it back." She flipped and started swearing, spitting, and kicking me in the shins. Now, our therapist told me I had two options when these circumstances arose. One was to tackle Rosey, take her to the ground, and hold her there until it passed. Or two: ignore her. Number one was my favorite, but since this was a public place and there were lots of cameras, not to mention Bob Hope, I opted for number two. Rosey did not like to be ignored. She refused to get in the car and threatened to walk the twenty miles home. The police intervened and she finally got inside. I decided it was time to freeze her out. After sitting silently at the opposite end of the limo for two minutes staring out the window, I felt a rush of air just before her $25,000 one-of-a-kind Chanel purse that I'd tracked down in France after she'd seen it in *Vogue* magazine came smashing into the side of my skull. It hurt like hell and I felt like doing a takedown right then and there, but I opted for the "I'm so sad and hurt that you would abuse me in this way after all I went through as a child" treatment. It worked. She calmed down. She apologized. I accepted. We laughed, went home, ordered Chinese, made love, ordered pizza, and went to sleep. The next morning we couldn't wait to get to the studio to tell John Goodman, Laurie Metcalf, and the others about our hilarious evening.

Roseanne has talked about this; she did have something like twenty-seven personalities. Only two of them liked me. It's true. I was there when she was "channeling." Her face and voice would literally morph into someone else. One personality was a four-year-old named Cindy, whom I really liked. She'd put on a ballerina outfit and just dance around. She even took dance lessons. Cindy did. Roseanne couldn't dance a lick. I know it's confusing, but Cindy was just so darn nice to me. I really enjoyed her company. It was much better to be with my little plus-sized Jon Benet than one of Rosey's many raving, shrew-type personalities who hated my guts. So I'd "call out" little Cindy, which I found out later during family week at the nut barn is something you're not supposed to do. Cindy spoke like a little kid and you could play with her. Unlike most of the others, she didn't bite or spit. She was fun and sweet. Regular Rosey would get crabby and I'd say, "Where's Cindy? Does Cindy want to come out and play?" It's insane, I know. At night, though, it got even weirder. Rosey had one personality that was a prostitute, and she'd want to get out and hit the bricks at two in the morning. One time Rosey got in the car as one personality, drove to Barstow, then turned into another that couldn't drive and could barely read. So I had to get dressed and go find her. I think the insanity eventually just wore me down. I'm a bit ashamed of myself for that, because she hung in there with me during my drug craziness. It's just that she just got so damn mean. So often. But I tried. I tried really hard.

In the summer of '93 I'd started working on my first really big movie, *True Lies*, and was out of town a lot. Rosey was happy for me but not happy about my absences. Her show filmed in L.A. and we'd never been apart and she freaked. She wanted me to quit the film. I knew that she was dealing with a lot of childhood issues, but there was no way I was walking out of this movie.

It was about this time our production company hired a new receptionist for my office, Kim Silva. My days usually started with Roseanne storming in, yelling at me, breaking a bunch of stuff, then storming out. I was used to it, but it shocked Kim. One day, I was on my hands and knees picking up a pile of glass shards that used to be a writing award. Kim came in to help and said, "You don't deserve to be treated this way."

I was stunned! "Who do you think you are? How dare you say that about my wife!"

Kim apologized and left and I broke down because I knew that she was right and I knew that it probably wasn't going to get better. I also knew that I had a new friend.

People in the media started saying that Kim, my pretty, young, slender assistant (that's what the papers always called her), and I were having an affair because she spent so much time with me and Roseanne. And because Kim was pretty, young, and slender. Roseanne came up with the idea that we'd have this three-way marriage to play on that. The three of us actually made it official on New Year's Eve 1993 on *The David Letterman Show*. Larry "Bud" Melman officiated. By then, Rosey and Kim had become buddies, too. The girls (Rosey, Kim, and Kami, Rosey's pretty, young, slender assistant) would go on vacation together, take naked pictures of one another, and send them back to me, and I'd be like, "OK, this is fun!" Guess which ones I kept the longest? Then it started getting weird. Well, weirder. Our marriage had been in trouble for a while and we knew it. Roseanne would try to make the best of it. Like at my third sober birthday. I was blindfolded, taken to a hotel room, and these two Heidi Fleiss girls were there. They had sex with each other and this pink thing that looked like a vibrating camel's nose. Roseanne and I had talked about what it would be like to see a show like this (complete with the vibrating camel nose). OK, I talked about it. I talked about it a lot. The ladies asked me to join them, but I said no. I only stayed about ten minutes, because I loved my wife (I thought it was a trap). I then ran upstairs to my room, where Roseanne had built a giant cake. She jumped out of it, looking pretty good herself, but she was pissed: "I'm angry that you watched those women have sex." And I said, "Yeah, but see, you set it up." And she said, "I know, but I'm still mad." She was mad for about six weeks. I spent a lot of time with Cindy.

Kim, Roseanne, and I were getting close. Very close. Is it considered cheating on your wife if she is there? I was on the set of *True Lies* in Washington, D.C., and a limo pulled up. The chauffeur told me there's a couple of ladies in the back that would love to say hi. It was Roseanne and Kim and they were dressed like twins. (Hey, Arnold Schwarzenegger and Danny De Vito were supposed to be twins, too.) They had matching leather Cat Woman–type outfits on and they said that they wanted to take me to the hotel and put on a little show. Hell, yeah!

The "show" consisted of me getting stripped down to the old boxers, blindfolded, and tied up to the bedposts while they danced around topless and tickled me. They weren't topless at first, but I suggested it since I couldn't see anyway. Of course I could see. Then I suggested that they could maybe do something more to my crotch region than just tickle it. This is when it got good. Rosey and Kim were excited because I couldn't see who was doing what. I was excited because I could.

I was so pleased that I told them I had to make it up to them and I would give each a massage. Naked. Everybody. Sweet. I thought, *I wonder if this is how the hip L.A. marriages work?* I hoped that we could do this again sometime. And we did. Only without Roseanne. I know that's fucked and I know that I lied about it on Howard Stern and I am very sorry, but by then Rosey was paying her future husband, Ben Thomas, to strip naked in gay biker bars and talk to dudes. Got him a new Harley for doing it. Kim was there, too. I couldn't believe that Kim didn't tell me until after Rosey and I officially broke up: "It wouldn't have been appropriate, Tom." "Kim, what the hell does being appropriate have anything to do with anything that's been going on in our lives then or now?!"

I could write about the many nights that Roseanne and I came home from work, had a nice dinner with the kids, then sat around and talked and laughed and watched a good movie. But who wants to read about that crap?

Instead, I'll tell you about the time Rosey pulled out my new hair transplants at the hospital. Although she had more than her share of surgeries, Roseanne hated for me to go under the knife. She wasn't really worried about me, she just wanted to know that she could have my full attention, and that's hard to give when you've just had a big chunk of your scalp removed. Plus, when I took pain pills I had a little trouble "standing at attention." I think you gentlemen know what I'm talking about.

I'd had several hair transplants, but I guess this time the procedure was taking a little longer than normal and Rosey didn't like to be kept waiting. Especially a hungry Rosey. The doctor had just finished tightly wrapping a gauze turban around my skull in order to keep the $25,000 worth of new hairs in place when the little woman stormed the operating room and yanked two handfuls (about $15,000 worth), not counting the stitches, out of my noggin. I cried, but in fairness the doctor cried first. Two hours later, I'm restitched and rewrapped and we're back in love at the Cheesecake Factory. Then we took advantage of my completely necessary pain pill high, stopping by Sunset Tattoo. This decision would cost me months of physical discomfort brought on by postdivorce tattoo removal surgery. It was worth it because, frankly, you'll never get laid with your ex-wife's face on your chest. Especially mine. She had "Property of Tom Arnold" on her butt, which, of course, made me the fourth largest property owner in California.

If I ever had to go to war, I'd definitely want Roseanne by my side. Partly because she'd be a great comrade in arms, but mostly so I could keep my eye on her. She'd be a ruthless enemy. Trust me.

Back in the good old days if someone crossed me, they crossed Roseanne, and vice versa. Which is why I got into numerous fights when we went out in public because some asshole started singing, "Ooh, say, can you see!" Which is also why I showed up at *Paramount Studios* to beat up Arsenio Hall. Arsenio was just the first of many feuds we nurtured. They usually started with some sort of broadcast fat jokes, but all of them, Arsenio, Howard Stern, everybody at *ABC*, ended up with truces and hugs all around for the home viewing audience to enjoy. Why is it that the people who criticize you the most are the ones you want approval from the most?

One feud Roseanne and I had with the paparazzi worked itself out in the court system after an amusing little incident at LAX. It was soon after Roseanne's national anthem triumph. As we got off the plane, a swarm of these intrusive bastards impeded our stroll through the airport. Finally Rosey had had enough: "Get 'em, honey." So as any white knight would do to defend the honor of his damsel in distress, I flipped out and chased these cockbrains through Terminal 4, tackling each of them and breaking all their cameras.

All but one. The one who took all of the pictures of me attacking and breaking all their cameras. The attack that led me to the L.A. DA's office. But I was lucky, because I had a first-class witness and Rosey would tell the authorities how the photogs incited me by bumping into us with their hard steel cameras and making offensive and derogatory comments about my little woman.

But I started to prepare for jail when at the hearing my star and only witness changed her story six times, finally deciding that she shouldn't even be there since she "didn't really see what happened." Fortunately, the photographers, after being very well compensated, dropped the charges. But to Roseanne's credit, she did stand shoulder to shoulder with me during the infamous Battle of the Parking Space against the *Seinfeld* cast.

Roseanne, *The Jackie Thomas Show*, and *Seinfeld* all filmed on the same lot, *CBS/MTM* in Studio City. And all of us big stars had our own parking space with our own name on it. Which is why I became very frustrated when someone else parked in mine. It was a huge pain in the ass to call security (actually, I never personally called security, but I did have to call someone and tell them to do it, so it was still a moderate pain in the ass) and have the car removed. On the fourth day in a row of being violated, I took matters into my own hands.

Clint Eastwood, one of my many idols, once rammed his pickup into a car that infiltrated his territory at Warner Brothers and I considered doing that, but with a new, mint-condition '57 Bel Air convertible and all, I decided an ugly note might work just as well. So I wrote: "How fucking stupid are you? Can't you fucking read? Keep your car out of my fucking spot. Love, Tom Arnold." Direct and to the point. During rehearsal, security came in and said that they had located the offender and that I could move my car into its rightful and much-deserved home.

Normally, I would have my assistant do this kind of dirty work, but I wanted to see for myself just what kind of a jackass

I was dealing with here. As my golf cart (I couldn't walk; it must've been fifty feet) approached the scene, a crowd had gathered including *Seinfeld's* own Jason Alexander. He told me that his lovely costar, Julia Louis-Dreyfus, had been the scoundrel who took my spot. He also said that she wanted to speak to me. She stepped forward with my note in her hand, and before she could apologize I said, "Hey, don't worry about it; it's OK. I had no idea it was you."

"But it's not OK," she shot back. "I'm offended by your note."

This may have been the worst apology I'd heard in my life. So I said, "That's too bad, because I'm offended by you parking in my fucking space!"

Jason and the rest of the *Seinfeld* posse, while hiding safely behind Ms. Louis-Dreyfus, got nervous, and she and her support group scurried away. Leaving me to ponder aloud, "The nerve of that arrogant bitch! I must report this to Rosey immediately." So I golf-carted to Stage 2, told my tale, and Rosey wanted blood. With the help of Laurie Metcalf and John Goodman, a plan of retaliation was devised. (The set of a television show can be a boring place to work, so you have to invent your own fun.)

Roseanne carried out the counterattack fifteen minutes later when her limo (she couldn't be trusted with a golf cart) pulled up to Julia's car and America's favorite mom climbed out, wrote "Julia Louis-*Drypuss*" in soap on the windshield, and left a picture of a big man's naked ass under the wiper. *Seinfeld* cocreator Larry David still has John Goodman's good side framed in his office.

Revenge was sweet until word spread around town. The papers loved the story. Even Billy Crystal did jokes about it at the Oscars. Jerry Seinfeld was cool: "You and me don't have a problem, do we, Tom?"

"Heck no, Jerry."

But I knew it had to end when Jack Nicholson came up to me at the *People's Choice Awards* and asked about it. I told him that it was all a joke and he said that if it was supposed to be funny, I should make it funny real fast and move on. Turns out this Julia Louis-Dreyfus is a much-loved and respected individual who just happened to treat me like dirt. That happens. So after we did an episode of *Jackie Thomas* about it, all was forgiven and forgotten.

Epilogue to this story. I asked for volunteers from *The Jackie Thomas Show* because I wanted to stockpile some bare-assed Polaroids for future parking violators. Everybody had fun with it, but a couple years later the guy who actually took the pictures filed a lawsuit. I think he wanted like a million dollars for his "pain and humiliation." He seemed pain-and-humiliation-free as he snapped away at the several female volunteers, including my lovely assistant, Kim. And I sensed no humiliation at the end of the season when he wrote me a nice thank-you letter and asked that I hire him back next year because he "appreciated the opportunity and loved working" for me.

But my show got canceled, so we were all looking for work, and when I didn't hire him to work my next show he hired a lawyer. I know that anytime you have naked asses in the workplace you're looking for trouble, but we do comedy, dammit, and these were frickin' volunteer naked asses, so I wanted to fight this one all the way to the United States Supreme Court! (And then write a show about it.) But Rosey and I were in the middle of one of *Entertainment Tonight's* "Top Ten Ugliest Hollywood Divorces" of all time and I gave the litigious little weasel $125,000 to go away.

Dad, Were You Ever a Daddy a Long, Long Time Ago?

Well, handsome, I was a stepdaddy for a while. I always considered it an honor that Roseanne trusted me with her TV show. A lot of her blood, sweat, and tears (literally) went into *Roseanne*. It was all about her life. But she trusted me with her real life, too, her kids. It takes a lot to trust someone with your children. How many people would you let load all of your valuables, jewelry, cash, and stocks, and the deed to your home into their car and drive away? Not many. So imagine the trust and respect needed to allow another human being into every aspect of your children's lives.

I knew it was an awesome responsibility. Jake (eleven), Jennifer (thirteen), and Jessica (fourteen) were good kids, but their lifestyles with Roseanne made the Osbournes look like the Cleavers. Like their mom, they were smart and funny and surprisingly loving free spirits. But teenage girls plus free spirits equals trouble. The kids' parents had been having marriage problems for a few years before they broke up, and Roseanne had to work on the road a lot. I think Roseanne felt guilty about this, so she cut the kids a lot of slack.

Slack meaning that there were no household rules. No curfew,

127

no school if they didn't feel like it. No boundaries, either. If they wanted to wear their mom's clothes, they just walked into her closet, picked out what they liked, and cut it up to fit them. When the girls argued, "fuckin' bitch" was the nicest thing they called each other. If they weren't happy they'd paint their bedroom walls black. Windows, too. The sinks were stained with black hair dye. Cigarette burns everywhere.

Now this crap may fly in a trailer park in Denver, but I considered it a little inappropriate in a $3 million house in Beverly Hills. "I considered it inappropriate" sounds a little arrogant coming from Mom's younger, mullet-headed boyfriend. An on-again, off-again drug addict with no experience raising children whatsoever. But the kids accepted me. Jake first. The boy was starved for attention. So every day after work, we played tennis and basketball for a couple of hours. This started from day one, when I was still trying to figure out what my role in the family would be. "Coach" sounded good. The kids had known me for years as Mom's "buddy," so this seemed like a natural transition. But the girls would not be so easy to coach. I learned that back in Iowa at the YWCA softball league. So I initiated Rule Number One: Everybody had to treat Mother with respect (i.e., "fuck off" was no longer a proper response to queries from the woman who gave you life).

The girls were in shock. How dare I alter the very essence of their relationship with dear old Mom! Now we needed some consequences. Violators would lose phone privileges (900 numbers were out altogether). Repeat offenders were grounded. Surprisingly, this new structure worked, partly because the kids saw that I openly and affectionately cared for their mother but mostly because children thrive on this shit.

They needed to have rules and consequences. Something easy to rebel against. So I made some more rules. Everybody had to go to school every day "and you'd better not try calling in another bull-crap bomb threat, Jenny." Once I got Jake to start showering more than occasionally we were rolling. Now we had curfews (curfews varied depending on age). We cleaned our own rooms. We smoked outside. We didn't throw butts in the pool anymore and we stayed the hell out of Mom's closet. There were some bumps along the way. The kids started stealing my clothes, but we worked through it.

Lying, punching, pinching, and spitting were all punishable by law. Standing in the middle of the living room and screaming, *"La-la-la I can't hear you!!!"* could get you grounded. Right, Jenny? The kids were doing well, and I was loving it. I went to all the parent-teacher conferences. If there was trouble at school, I showed up. This is how Jessica and I bonded. We had a little tag team action versus a federal judge and his mouthy fourteen-year-old daughter.

Fewer and fewer of our family therapy sessions were being broken up by storm-outs. We were starting to make it through the whole hour! By now, each kid had his or her own set of rules and consequences laminated and framed outside his or her bedroom (brightly colored bedroom) door. And we accomplished all of this before I got clean and sober. When I was in rehab, the family started backsliding. I got many emergency phone calls: "Jessica's locked in her room and she won't come out"; "Tom, Mom's acting crazy again"; "Jenny lit her rug on fire." Girls, girls, girls.

I patched things up as best I could between group therapy sessions, and when I came out I was ready to rock. The first thing I discovered after my reemergence was that I wasn't the only one with a drug problem. So Jessica went into drug rehab, Jenny went into food rehab, and Jake and I studied Judaism.

Looking back, I was pretty tough, but those kids worked as hard on themselves as any adults I'd ever known. They all even went, separately, to a sixty-day Outward Bound program in Utah. I highly recommend this kind of program, especially for privileged kids with body issues. For two months they had to hike ten miles every day in the desert, build their own shelter, find their own water, make their own food, and start their own fires using two sticks and a piece of twine. All this with little or no supervision (as far as the kids knew). I figured Jake would breeze through this. He did, losing twenty pounds. Jessica, a Goth and *The Cure* groupie who used lots of dark makeup and only wore black or red velvet, had a tougher time. But Jess pulled it off, too, losing thirty pounds and gaining some more self-esteem.

Now, Jenny was the stubborn one. I was worried because I could easily see her sitting down in the middle of the desert and giving up, telling the peers that were trying to pressure her to "fuck off and die." I know it sounds harsh, but this was Jenny's version of "have a nice day." We were amazed when we didn't get any emergency phone calls telling us that Jenny had beaten the counselors senseless and escaped to Salt Lake City for some ice cream.

On the last day of the trek, the families fly into this beautiful Rocky Mountain gorge where we gather at a finish line. The kids, only a half-mile away, are told that their families are here to take them back to civilization and are waiting around the bend and five miles straight ahead. We watch as the first and fastest (Jake was first when he went) kid comes whipping around the corner and spots his family straight ahead. This is the most exciting and emotional thing you'll ever see. The kids are thinner and filthier than you've ever seen them. And they run into their parents' arms and everybody's crying. Kid after kid comes by and still no Jenny. Finally we see a girl winding toward us and she's picking up steam. But we don't recognize her because she's forty pounds lighter and smiling! And when she runs into our (me, Mom and her dad, Bill) arms you'd think we'd all won the Olympics. That feeling has to be the best part of being a parent, because no matter what happens, all of these kids now know that they can take care of themselves. With two sticks and a piece of twine. Sadly, being the enablers we were, our gift to Jenny was a big bag of candy bars. Half-eaten, of course.

That night, we did these family exercises where we walked on wires forty feet up between telephone poles, trying to overcome our fear of heights (after what the kids went through, we had to do it). Then we did this exercise in trust. Where we fell backward ten feet into somebody's arms. The kids' dad, Bill, was picked to catch me. God knows why, but he caught me. Maybe because he knew I never bad-mouthed him in front of his kids or maybe because he could tell that I openly and affectionately cared for his children.

When Roseanne and I broke up in 1994 she asked the kids not to talk to me, and they haven't really except for the time I ran into Jenny once at the studio. She looked great and I told her so. We had a brief but very pleasant conversation. The next day, Roseanne threatened to file a restraining order. Other than a couple of covert phone calls from the kids, I have had absolutely no contact. That was tough. They meant a lot to me. I wrote them each a good-bye letter that fall. I don't know if Roseanne gave the letters to them, but what I said was: Thank you. Thank you for letting me be a part of your lives for almost five years. Thank you for the lessons I learned. Thank you for the hugs and "I love yous." I'm sorry for the way things turned out. I'm sorry for the mistakes I made. You all were my first real family, and now as I start another, I hope that we have as many laughs and half as many tears as we did. (Remember when I was yelling and I sat down too hard and my big ass broke through the pool chair and got stuck in it, Jess? Jake, remember when I got scared and kicked the karate instructor in the nuts? Jenny, remember when you stole my new size 13 crocodile shoes and you left them in the driveway and they were ruined when I ran over them with the car?) And when my daughter turns eighteen, if she's real, real good, maybe we'll get tattoos together, too.

Daddy, Are You and the Funny
TV Lady Still Friends?

No, not anymore, foxy, but I remember in early April of 1989, when Rosey and I first "got together," she said, "Give me five years to help get my kids better, get me better, and help me fix my show, and I'll make you a big star." She was stoned and I thought she was just being insecure. I knew that if we got married it would be forever. But about five years later to the day, April 15, 1994, she filed for divorce. Coincidence? Well, if it was some Hollywood deal with the devil then I want my soul back, because I ain't a "big star" (Cruise, Hanks). She did help me enormously. And she believed in me. Whatever confidence I have as a performer I owe to her, because unlike almost everybody else back then, she thought I was funny. Experts will one day point to this as the beginning of her mental illness. I thought that if someone as talented and brilliant as Roseanne thought I was funny it must be true. But the sad truth is it took our breakup and *True Lies* to convince people that the crazy broad might have been on to something.

The day the laughter died I arrived at the studio to shoot my *CBS* television show, *Tom*. Roseanne was standing outside my office with the security guards and a pile of my stuff she broke.

Nothing unusual about that. She tried to throw me off the lot, but the guards explained that she couldn't because I was there to shoot *my* show. This would've been so much easier for her if she hadn't let me get my own TV show in the first place. Later that night, while we shot in front of the studio audience, a man walked up in the middle of a scene and handed me divorce papers. In spite of the warning signs, I was stunned. My credit cards were canceled, I was locked out of my house, and all my clothes were floating in the pool. Someone even killed my fish. What kind of a sick bitch kills a fella's fish?

The press went crazy. Roseanne made some horrible and untrue accusations. I guess she thought this would be easier if I was the monster and she was the victim. I never hit her. Well, once I backhanded her in the stomach, but she *was* strangling me. Although I *was* on drugs at the time, so I definitely deserved it. My favorite Roseanne quote was when she said she fled to Europe, fearing for her life, after hearing what O.J. did to his wife. Now, unless I'm confusing psychic with psychotic this would've been impossible, since the woman "fled" for Europe at the end of April and O.J. lost his chance to ever be in another *Naked Gun* movie on June 6.

But the truth about our breakup was sad enough: we just plain wore out. We both tried with everything we had, but we couldn't do it anymore. It wasn't meant to be. With Roseanne, everything was black or white. You were either a genius or an idiot. A god or the devil (think borderline personality disorder). Now I was Lucifer and I was banished from her kingdom. Make no mistake about it, Roseanne tried to destroy me and my career. She called my parents, network presidents, anybody and everybody she could think of that might actually have a positive feeling or two about Old Tom. One week later she called me and apologized for saying and doing those vicious things. Then she called the press and took it all back. She tore up the divorce papers. Thank God I was every bit as crazy as she was! So, I shut down my show and we flew to our farm in Iowa to give it the old "one last try." We agreed that we loved each other and if we ever did break up, we'd stay friends and it would be civil. No more crazy shit like sending out libelous press releases or serving me divorce papers while I'm taping my sitcom, and under no circumstances would anyone kill anybody's fish. That kind of stuff scares the kids, for God's sake.

Things went well until I had to go back to work and Roseanne had to "flee" to Europe. She said that I wasn't "available enough" to her (the nine-hour time difference didn't help), and in May, in the middle of my final show of the season, I got served with divorce papers again. A new shit storm had begun. But for once in my life I laid low. I never bad-mouthed her. I wasn't ready to hate her. I went back home to Iowa for a couple of weeks.

So Rosey was in Europe with Ben Thomas (her chauffeur and bodyguard), who later became her third husband. He was a nice guy. I had even hired the big bastard (six-four, 240 pounds). Took him away from his career at the doughnut shop (a small step above the meatpacking plant). I got a call from Alan Smith of the *National Enquirer* saying that Ben and Rosey were "together"!

"Together, together?"

"Together, together."

But I had to see it for myself. Even though we were separated, I really didn't believe we'd ever get divorced. I figured Rosey would calm down and come back like usual.

Remember, I was used to her disappearing. Sometimes just her personalities would change and other times she would disappear altogether. Toward the end of our marriage this was almost a nightly occurrence (why always at night? It really fucked up *SportsCenter* for me) and it was at least confusing and stressful. But most of all, it was damn hard to make dinner plans. Rosey occasionally disappeared in the house or in the neighborhood. Sometimes to various locations around Southern California, but *always* in her head. This Europe thing was new and now she had an accomplice. An accomplice I'd sent to an Israeli Special Operations school to master the lethal art of hand-to-hand combat. So I was kinda fucked.

But I phoned my travel agent anyway, told him to keep it quiet, because I wanted to surprise Rosey, and I booked a place to stay near where she and Jethro were summering in Sardinia. So we (me and my brother Gay Chris) caught the next plane to Italy. As soon as Gay Chris and I and our Roman bodyguard, Rocky, drove out of the airport, three cars full of stinky Italian dudes pulled us over. And they've all got machine guns. It's her "people." I've just got the one "person," so again I'm screwed again. They knew that I was coming because of the soon-to-be-fired travel agent. They took us to Rosey's villa. Of course, the guy from the *National Enquirer* was there, too, camera in hand (actually, I should've seen this coming; he was on the plane with me and Gay Chris). He captured the whole beautiful reunion. His very presence probably saved me from at least a pretty severe beat-down. Ben looked pissed. Rosey looked guilty. She asked why I was there.

"A little R and R," I say. I asked if she was screwing Ben.

She said, "No," but she was looking down, so I knew she was lying. I felt this kind of weird relief because, you know what, it was over and she was going to be fine. Ben would be there for her, as I had been during her last divorce.

We vacated the immediate vicinity, but my brother, Rocky, and I stayed on Sardinia for a couple more days. It was beautiful. The last night, Rocky, a bit of a male chauvinist, informed me that under Italian law I could legally have Ben killed and he could arrange it, because, technically, "he is screwing your wife."

"No thanks, Rock," I said. Then I started thinking about Ben. I could deal with him stealing my wife away from me with his boyish charm, but when I thought about the big lug cruising around in my '57 Bel Air convertible I got real pissed and decided that he could not get off so easy (not that the next eight years of Ben's life would be easy). So I said to Rock, "Anything else maybe we could do?" and Rock answered, "Do you want him to go to prison for a long time?"

"No, that would be bad; he'd be gone and Rosey might want to reconcile. How about we give him a little scare?" I said. I was indignant because the man was doin' my old lady before she filed her papers. But more important than that was the fact that he was gonna be layin' his big sweaty ass on my side of the bed, the good side of the bed, the side of the bed with the built-in super secret control panel (it could've come right off the Starship *Enterprise*) that operated everything electrical in the house, and he'd be watching the seventy-inch drop-screen TV I'd just installed. So I coughed up $10,000 and when Ben tried to clear customs in Rome eight "police officers" swarmed down on him (well, now, he started it!) and Ben, the user of all my cool stuff, was searched thoroughly, and I do mean *thoroughly*. I made sure they left Rosey alone, but the poor kids missed their flight. Darn-it! I laughed to myself about my evil revenge for the next few months (couldn't really tell anybody; I mean it's probably kinda illegal) until one day I picked up *People* magazine and saw a picture of the happy couple, cruising down Sunset in the world's most beautiful '57 Bel Air convertible.

On July 14, Rosey got back from Europe. The day before, I had moved out of the house with practically only the clothes on my back (she'd burned the rest of them) and of course I took all of the toilet paper (creating Ben's first errand) and whatever toiletries I could fit in my trunk (I'm still using some of the cream rinse). *True Lies* opened that day. My professional life instantly changed. I did well in a blockbuster movie. Nobody expected it, most of all me. But nobody could ever take it away from me. My TV show had been canceled. I was obviously not welcome on the *Roseanne* set, where I had worked for the last six years. Everybody thought my career was over. I couldn't read the paper or watch the late-night talk shows because the jokes were just brutal.

But this movie came out and a lot of people loved me in it. It was amazing. Incredible. The brilliant director James Cameron made it happen. *Fox*, the studio, didn't want me. I almost didn't go to the audition because I didn't want to waste Jim's time. But I wanted to meet him, so I went so I could say I did, and he said, "While you're here, why don't you read?"

"Read what?" I asked.

Then he went, "The pages you were supposed to memorize for your audition."

"Oh yeah, that would've been smart, huh?"

So he handed me the pages and I read, rather poorly, but the future "King of the World" asked if he could film me, and I'm like "sure," and he does. Then he says he wants Arnold Schwarzenegger to come in to read with me. I was like this can't be happening. Arnold was my hero. I'd met him once at Planet Hollywood but didn't really know him. Now Arnold came in and it instantly clicked. I loved the guy and I got the fucking job! Jim asked me not to tell anyone for two weeks. I tried to keep quiet, but I couldn't. I still can't keep a secret about myself, good or bad. Fortunately, as usual, nobody believed me.

The Sunday after *True Lies* knocked off the great *Forrest Gump* to open at number one, I got a call from Roseanne. She said she heard about the movie and she felt she should be a part of it. She was right. She went on to say that she wanted us to try again. "What about Ben?" I asked.

"It's not his fault." She was right again.

I still cared for her, but I had been burned too bad. I agreed to go to therapy with her the next week to try to at least be friends. Her kids called me; they were happy that we were "acting like adults for a change." I was happy, too. We went to therapy once. After two hours of the most intense session we ever had, she stood up and said, "This is going to be too hard to put back together," and she walked out. She was right one last time. That night I heard she had an "I hate Tom" tattoo cover-up party, which more than likely created an international ink shortage. We have not spoken face-to-face since that day. Over eight years ago.

Daddy, Have People in Hollywood Always Loved You?

Not really, angel. I am the only person in Hollywood history who was ever booed at the *Golden Globes*. In 1996, I was presenting an award with the gorgeous Teri Hatcher (TV's Lois Lane) and as usual I was having trouble reading the TelePrompTer when she jokingly interrupted, saying, "Maybe I should read," to which I jokingly said, "OK, but it's probably not what you do best." Let the booing commence.

I was immediately shunned by my own community. No one would speak to me except George Clooney, who stated the obvious: "Nice work, Tom; now every woman in this room hates you." But I was only joking! The next day on *The Today Show*, Al Roker slammed me and Maria Shriver was forced to defend me: "He was only joking, Al; that's how Tom is." I hate to hurt feelings, so I sent flowers to Teri with my apology. I heard her husband wanted to kick my ass. I even sent an apology note to Dick Clark, who produced the show. He wrote a nice letter back telling me not to worry about it. At least Dick Clark gets it.

I didn't hear back from Teri Hatcher until three years later when I was at *Saturday Night Live's 25th Anniversary Show*. They'd invited all the former hosts to attend, and David Spade

141

came up to me with Alyssa Milano and said hi. Alyssa's seat was right in front of mine and I was teasing her a little about the size of her dress ("nice doily") when she turned around and said, "Hey, Tom, haven't you done enough to me?" That is the moment when I realized that it was not Alyssa Milano but, in fact, a very trim and youthful-looking Teri Hatcher I'd been teasing. Me and my big mouth!

A few months later I was asked to play a part opposite Jon Tenney, a fine actor and husband of Teri, in the underrated *Fox TV* show *Get Real*. I was nervous, but he was great and unless he thought I was Alyssa Milano, all seemed to be forgiven and forgotten. Once again.

Daddy, Did You Have a Grampaw and Granma Like I Do?

Yes, big shooter, and if I hadn't had the grandparents I did, I might have grown up to be a loser. OK, shithead, an even bigger loser. Every kid needs someone to throw the ball around with. Someone who will teach them the right rules and take them to the big games. Games so big that you could not possibly sleep the night before. You stood at the end of your driveway, University of Iowa Hawkeye hat in hand, starting at the crack of dawn. Was it the football that was so exciting?

Our team wasn't even close to being good. Maybe it was the two-hour drive to Iowa City, the snack on the way, the peanuts and hot dogs and frosty malts at the game? Or was it the three-hour drive back home to Ottumwa through tractor traffic with a welcome pit stop at a beautiful Packwood, Iowa, oasis called Dickey's Prairie Home's all-you-can-eat buffet. A place with food so tempting that I literally became a man there when I was only seven. After I enjoyed my fourth or fifth plate, the owner slid over to our booth, picked up our ticket, and scratched out "child" and wrote "adult" and slammed the check down. They'd had enough.

But the real reason I couldn't sleep, the real reason I got so

143

excited, was because I got to spend time with my grandpa Tom Graham. Tom was a man's man. He played sports (nickname: Gashouse Graham) and was a bit of a legend in Southeast Iowa. He umpired and refereed over 3,500 high school and college basketball, baseball, and football games.

Yes, Tom was a man's man. If you cut off Tom Graham in traffic, you got the finger. If you honked at him, he'd ask you to step out of your car: "Come on, young fella; put 'em up." But I always felt safe with Tom, even when he'd occasionally pass nine or ten cars around a blind curve, lights flashing, horns blowing, if we were late for Dickey's. Or at the barber's, he'd be sitting in the chair getting his weekly butch, acting like he was reading *Field and Stream* when I could clearly see in the mirror behind Tom that inside *F and S* was good old *Playboy*.

He and the barber, Bill the Butcher, would say, "Look at the size of those guns, Tom."

"Yeah, now those are some big-ass fish, Bill."

I played dumb because I was just happy to see even the reflected glory of Miss Jayne Mansfield or Janet Pilgrim. It would be many years before I would see a real live naked woman that wasn't my grandma. Many, many years.

Tom worked at John Morrell Meats for fifty years, and he was married to my grandma Dort (short for Dorothy, although we probably should've called her Dorth). Tom was the first to pass away. Tom had diabetes and his last couple years were tough ones thanks to a broken kneecap at the ice-skating rink and fingers severed while cleaning under the lawn mower as it was still running: "Forgot to turn the bastard off, Tommy!" The last time I saw him, he was in the hospital after having a stroke. I was nervous as my buddy Mike Sporer and I arrived. Nervous that Tom would be in pain or look different. Nervous that he'd somehow not be the man I'd grown up with.

But I was relieved when I walked into his room. He was sitting up, barking out orders, looking good: "Hey, Tommy, Mike, how are you boys doing? Can you believe this bullshit?" (pointing at the wires and fancy hospital machines). All was well, I thought, and Tom said, "Mike, how's Fred?" (Mike's dad who had worked at the slaughterhouse for Tom twenty-five years before).

"He's good, Tom."

"Hard worker," Tom said. "Doesn't screw around like he used to. Tommy, what are you up to these days?"

"Well, besides college?" I asked.

"You're in college, Tommy?"

At first I thought he was kidding me. Then I looked into his eyes and my heart sank. He didn't remember. He'd lost all his memories of the last ten to fifteen years. So with a huge lump in my throat and the look of fear in his eyes I retraced the last decade and a half. I felt sad for my grandpa. I felt scared for my grandma. And I felt sad and scared for me, too. I knew that this was just part of growing up, but that was the last thing I wanted to do.

Grandpa Tom passed away soon after, but I remember him not for that day but for all the other days when he took me hunting, fishing, and we played catch. And I cannot go to an Iowa football game and not think about me and Tom. I know I was one lucky kid.

I'll never forget the final words the priest spoke at the funeral: "Tom Graham was loved by his family and friends. Tom was a man's man, a sports man, and I think God is gonna call Tom *safe* [priest does "safe" umpire arm motion] in heaven." He'd have to.

The irony of the priest's comments was the fact that Tom's side of the family was Jewish. They hadn't practiced for a couple generations after his grandmother, Ma Cohen, realized that she and her sister, being the only Jews in an eighty-mile radius, would do better by their families if they assimilated. I didn't know any of this family history until after I had studied Judaism for nine months with my stepson. He was getting bar mitzvahed, and I was converting.

I was at my grandma Dort's funeral and one of Tom's cousins came over and handed me a big black book: "Thought you might be interested in this, Tommy." Inside were the details of the deep, dark family secret. That my mother's side of my family had Jewish blood. At first, I felt elated. This made so much sense. I'd converted not just to please my wife but to please myself, and now I knew that technically I was a "real Jew." Although in the eyes of God, once you convert, you are a real Jew and anyone who says any different is a frickin' sinner. But if you, like me, grew up a stepchild, the idea of having a bloodline that went straight to Moses, Jesus, and Barbra Streisand was pretty darn cool. After the initial excitement set in, I felt a little frustrated that no one had told me this earlier. Before I studied. Before I made the big donation to the Synagogue Art Fund (now I sound like a real Jew).

Every kid needs a Dort in their life. Someone who is always on their side. Someone who is patient and kind. Someone who bakes a lot. I was Dort's favorite grandkid. Tom told me. Every kid should be somebody's favorite. Dort worked at the Coca-Cola Bottling Factory for forty years. Quality control. Forty years of watching bottle after bottle whiz by on the conveyor belt. Scanning each and every one. Protecting the consumer from broken glass and mouse parts. "But mostly mouse parts," Dort would say.

Dort and Tom had a two-acre garden behind their house. They raised sweet corn, tomatoes, strawberries, green onions, cabbage, potatoes, carrots, radishes, watermelons, apples, pears. You name it. They spent twenty to thirty hours a week, eight months a year, working their garden, and they gave almost all of the food away. Maybe they knew the key to a good marriage. Lots of filthy, dirty, backbreaking manual labor. And separate bedrooms.

When Tom passed away, we were all worried about Dort, but

146

the truth is she came to life and, much like her roses, bloomed. At sixty-seven years old, Dort had never driven a car, so she got her license. Dort, a fifty-year smoker, gave up cigs and started exercising. Every day she walked seven and a half miles to the Senior Citizen Center and back (she didn't really trust the horseless carriage). Dort made friends. She went to Vegas on gambling bus trips. She was a modern woman. I'm happy that Dort got to see me have some success. We talked on the phone several times a week, and she watched everything I did that was on one of the three TV channels they got in Iowa.

But after ten good years, fifty years of smoking caught up with her. Emphysema is a terrible way to die. She went in the hospital and I tried to encourage her, but she didn't seem too worried about what was next. I told her that she was gonna live a long time. I bought her the new green leather recliner she'd wanted and I put it in her living room: "It's so beautiful, Dort. Hurry up and get out of here, so that you can sit in it." But as the weeks went on, the news from the doctors was worse and worse, so I moved the new big green leather recliner into her hospital room.

One Monday, I got a call from her doctor. He said that Dort had maybe twenty-four hours to live. I talked to her and told her I'd be right there. "Don't you have your show this week, Tommy?"

"Yeah, Dort, but it's OK; we'll shut it down."

"Absolutely not. Do your show first, then come on the weekend."

I said OK, but I felt guilty. I should've already been on a plane, but miraculously Dort held on, and I finished the show. I flew out Friday night to Iowa and went straight to the hospital. Dort, sitting in the green recliner, opened her eyes, looked up, hugged me as hard as anyone ever has, and said, "I'm so glad you made it, Tommy; no one in my life has ever taken care of me like you have." Hearing this made me feel happy. (I guess she really liked the new big green leather recliner).

Dort wasn't big on "I love you," but this was even better. It also made me sad. A good woman like Dort should have been well taken care of by a lot of people. She died the next week. For a year or so I still unconsciously picked up the phone to call her every time something big happened to me. Then one night, she came to me in my sleep and told me that everything was going to be all right. I woke up crying but at peace. I knew that somebody was giving my grandma the best care possible.

Immediately after the funeral, my Aunt Carolee, Dort's only living child, put Dort's house up for sale. But I wanted to go over there and be in it for a while and sit in the new big green leather recliner. You know, to think about Dort, Tom, and me. But buyers had already made a generous offer and my aunt couldn't wait, so I outbid them and bought the house. It was too soon to have strangers in my grandparents' place. I spent the next weekend there, like I had many times as a kid, looking around, remembering. It was sad and nice at the same time. I asked my parents to plant the garden, to keep it going. I finally sold the house a couple years later.

Dottie Arnold was married to D. B. Arnold for sixty years. Dottie was a fine actress, a three-time best actress winner with the Ottumwa Community Players. She brought me into the theater. At age four I played one of the Siamese kids in *The King and I.* At the end of our two-week run, this beautiful woman who played Anna, the teacher, signed my program and kissed me on the top of my head. I still love her. That very moment is why I am in show business today.

Dottie was unusual in my hometown in that she traveled, read, and was socially liberal (after all, she was in the theater). She worked at the First United Methodist Church, so of course I sang in the choir. I sang soprano solos in the choir until one Sunday I got a combination of stage fright and puberty in the middle of "Onward Christian Soldiers." I panicked as I mouthed words that weren't coming out. I was ashamed and embarrassed, but I'll never forget her smiling face sticking out of the confused Methodist mass. A face that let me know it was OK, I was still loved even as I humiliated myself publicly (that has really stuck with me). And there'd still be turkey pot pie at Dottie's house after church.

Since I had no mother around for a lot of my young life, Dottie considered herself my mom. As a kid, I didn't like that because: (1) she was too old; and (2) she wore funny hats. Dottie was one of those freaky ladies that wore a different hat every day. She actually had a little show about her hundreds of hats that she performed at women's clubs all over the tristate area.

Dottie was big on hugs and kisses and "I love you." Too big. It got a little sloppy. More than anybody else, she enjoyed my success. She'd say things like, "I'd love to fly first class just once," and, "I'd love to ride in a limousine just once." But every time I got her a limo she rode in the front seat because she felt bad for the driver. "He doesn't want you up there, Dottie," I'd say. Then she'd invite the poor bastard into her home and make him eat food. Now, Dottie was a good cook, but this was after she went blind. So you had to be a little careful.

She loved to read any newspaper or magazine articles that mentioned me, so I got her one of those reading machines that make each letter two feet tall. It would take her an afternoon just to read "untalented gold digger." But she persevered, God bless her.

Dottie enjoyed the hell out of Roseanne, as did all of my family. And Dottie always thanked her for my success. That's how my family is. They constantly praise the in-laws to the point of humiliating the out-laws. My family also doesn't take sides in a divorce if there are children involved. Why do we have a family again?

Anyway, Dottie liked Rosey, but when we broke up Dottie wrote me a letter (writing letters was harder than reading them for her, so this must have taken a month) and said that by giving

Rosey so much credit she had always sold me a little short. Dottie knew that I was going to do very well on my own. This made up for the letter, which I still have, that she sent me when I left the University of Iowa for Minneapolis and a stand-up comedy career. Basically, that letter said: "Get real, comedy is no career, come back home, and be a stockbroker before you embarrass yourself anymore." Too late.

Dottie used to make me so mad. Like the time in Detroit. We'd just seen *Miss Saigon* and she tried to tell me that a real helicopter landed in the theater when she saw the play in New York. I said, of course, that she was nuts and we argued in front of a crowd of people (you could never land a helicopter in the middle of a group of people like that), people who I'm sure were wondering why this jackass didn't just let it go for the sake of his dear sweet granny. Finally, Dottie slipped on the ice and fell and I was so concerned that the insignificant matter was immediately dropped. Until we got back to the hotel. My only explanation for our occasional combativeness was that in some ways I did think of her as a mother. Make sense? I don't know. . . .

Dottie's death was sudden. A massive heart attack. I told my therapist I was happy that at least Dottie died peacefully, during her nap. He told me that actually he was sure she was in incredible pain (thanks, fella). Her funeral was the saddest one I've been to. Being the oldest grandkid, I emceed (do you call it emceeing at a funeral?). Every single grandchild spoke and cried about his or her own special relationship with Dottie. That's the thing about her: she made everyone feel special. I also choked up and rambled on and on and finally closed with a story about looking down Dottie's nightgown at her boobs. Right story. Wrong room.

Anyway, I'm grateful that I spent so much of my life with Dottie. I always liked being with her. When I was two and a half, I ran away. Dottie, who lived four miles from Dad's house, saw me on her front porch and called my mom. Mom didn't even notice I was gone. I lived with Dottie and D.B. for a year when I was twelve, but I had to move out because she cried every time I got into a fight at school. She cried a lot. But I made it up to her. She was my date to the *True Lies* premiere. First-class airfare, limos everywhere, and a huge party in Westwood afterward. Dottie was lovin' it. We were hobnobbing with all these big shots when I felt a gust of wind. I looked up and a huge helicopter landed right in the middle of the party. I am such a jackass.

When Dottie passed away, Grandpa D.B. was devastated. He told me that his biggest regret was that he was "so damn crabby." He *was* crabby, and they did argue a lot. D.B. wasn't so much arguing as giving running commentary on Dottie's conversation: "Oh, great, she wants to spend more money, why not give everything to the goddamn church!" or, "Just like Hubert H. Humphrey, diarrhea of the mouth." That sorta thing. It was kinda like listening to the radio and a CD player at the same time, loudly, and you never knew who to look at. Fortunately, Dottie being blind and all took the pressure off.

I spent the least amount of time as a kid with D.B. He seemed to work a lot. D.B. was a very smart and serious man. He got his master's degree at twenty. He ran Social Services in our area for over thirty years. Tough job. Tough decisions. D.B. had that Depression disease where if you were raised during the Depression you thought that the economy could and would collapse at any moment. He died a millionaire wearing a holey T-shirt and a pair of old pants that the guy whose yard I used to mow had thrown out twenty years before. D.B. brought his own butter to restaurants because they charged ten cents for theirs. Dad said that toward the end of D.B.'s life he caught his dad changing the price tags at the grocery store. As a kid, if I visited him, D.B. would follow me around the house to make sure I didn't leave any lights on or the water running, which seemed crazy back then, but I find myself doing the exact same shit now.

He lived in a big old house and he hated to hire help, which is why he broke his hip falling off the third-floor roof while fixing the seldom-used air conditioner—seldom used because of the "skyrocketing cost of electricity." A week after he got out of the hospital (it took us four days to talk him into even going in), Dad was driving by D.B.'s house and saw him on the third-floor roof again lurching his walker around. Dad, horrified, hit the brakes, then thought, *That crazy bastard, what the hell*, and just kept driving. Sometimes, when you break your hip, they give you a bucket to pee in until you recover. D.B. found this to be very convenient and kept it long after it was necessary. When Dad caught him using the bucket in the perfume aisle at Drug Town, he pried the bucket out of his dear old dad's tobacco-stained hands. The parent officially became the child. I do not look forward to that day for me and my dad. But I know that it will happen. Hopefully not at Drug Town.

D.B. was not the poster boy for the American Lung Association. He chain-smoked unfiltered cigarettes for seventy years. He died at eighty-six with a cigarette (no brand name, too expensive, just "cigarette") in his hand and an open bottle of vitamins in front of him. One missing. The first vitamin he ever took killed the man, World War II could not.

I loved old D.B. When I moved to L.A. he secretly loaned me $5,000. He would always say that I was the only one who ever paid him back. That made me proud, but I have a feeling that I'm the only one he ever loaned to. I understood D.B. He hated the church because he was raised a "speaking in tongues" Pentecostal. His mother, Great-grandma—no one ever told me her name—lived with him and Dottie, and when they went out of town I got to baby-sit her and it was scary. A nine-year-old kid in this big old creaky house with spooky streetlights shining in the window, reflecting off the mirror on the dresser at the bottom of my bed in the shape of a killer. I never slept a wink. And I didn't dare open my eyes 'cause I'd see in the mirror the bad guy standing on the headboard above me ready to pounce. But since I was a brave little boy I still always watched out for my great-grandma . . . and for the man above the bed . . . and the cakes and cookie jars in the kitchen.

I much preferred baby-sitting the next-door neighbor kid. On Saturday nights I'd be doing the dishes (the kid that misbehaved the most during the week did the dishes on Saturday night; I always did the dishes on Saturday night) and I'd be watching the Howards get ready to go out and I'd be so excited when Mrs. Howard picked up the phone and dialed and I'd hear our phone ring and she'd ask me if I was available (man, was I available) and could I watch little Craig. Fifty cents an hour. Not too shabby. Sadly, they quit calling. I always wondered why until one day I caught Mr. Howard after a few beers and he told me they didn't ask me back because I was eating them "out of the goddamn house and home." I apologized. I did eat a lot because, unlike our house, their refrigerator had food in it. Good food. Pies and ice cream, and not just vanilla.

When I spoke at D.B.'s funeral I talked about why he was like he was. Not a fun childhood. Fifty years of hard work. A very chatty social butterfly of a wife and, of course, the war. D.B. was a decorated medic in World War II. D.B. had seen things that no man should ever have to see. He was in the Forty-second Rainbow Division, the first soldiers into Dachau, the concentration camp. He had to help clean it up. Dottie told me that he was never the same after that. Who could be? Although I could always get him talking about being in Hitler's lair and he'd show me the Nazi flags taken off the bodies of the "dirty Krauts" he'd shot "before they could shoot me," D.B. would never talk about the concentration camp. I guess going through something like that could make a man a little crabby.

Daddy, Did You Have a Good Daddy When You Were Born?

You bet I did, sugar bear. My dad, Jack Arnold, is the last one left. It scares me, but he is the final person alive who was there with me in the beginning. Before the glory. When I really needed somebody good in my life. When I was little. Under ten pounds. And I was young. Zero. I needed someone to take care of me. Not like now, when I can take care of myself by hiring people to hire other people to take care of me for me. But Dad was there and he was good. Real good.

How lucky am I? There's 5 billion people in the world, it's a crapshoot, and I won the lottery; I got the best on my very first try. Even at an early age, Dad was a superstar. Rookie of the year for sure. Consensus All-American, unanimous M.V.P. First-ballot Hall of Famer. Dad changed the game. I know it's hard to believe, but when I was born way back in 1959 most teams were two-man operations, father and mother. If they wanted any chance at all to win.

Dad was nineteen, pretty young, but his partner was only sixteen, too young, so he had to carry the team from the start. Why they chose me first a couple years later I'll never know, but that was my biggest break. Bigger than the writing job on *Roseanne,*

155

even bigger than Jim Cameron's movie. Of course, it took me many years to realize and appreciate my good fortune. But the signs were there early on.

We don't talk a whole hell of a lot now, but that's OK because of the attention and unconditional love I received from Dad starting day one. So much that I didn't appreciate it, which is how I will be to my children. I want to give them so much love that they take it for granted, too. Dad was the one who taught me that. Dad was fun to be around. He played with me. Games, cars, kites, hide-and-seek, you name it and he always made me laugh. Hard. He laughed hard, too.

And Dad was a busy guy. He had a big high-powered career. He ended up an industrial engineer but in the old days sold greeting cards, vacuum cleaners, and lawn mower blades door-to-door (all of these beat the heck out of his current retiree job of chauffeuring body parts from the hospital to the lab). He was even vice president of the Ottumwa Junior Chamber of Commerce, not to brag. He gave me so much that when I was four and his partner (we called her Mom) left, I never felt insecure. I knew that we still had our leader, and somehow I knew that everything would be OK. Isn't that unbelievable?

And Dad was subtle. He didn't lecture me about honesty. He was just honest. He didn't preach to me about responsibility. He just always was. He was good to people, so I knew that I should be good to people. To encourage them. To raise their spirits. I learned that in life there is a lot of gray area, but there is one absolute. One unwritten rule, if you will. You never, ever, under any circumstances, give up on your teammates. Especially the young ones. When Mom left, Dad could've become a free agent. He could've tested the open market. Who could blame him? He was young, twenty-five, lots of skills, in his prime, but he stayed home for less money, less exposure. He stayed loyal. To me (four) and the rookies (Lori, three; Scotty, one).

And amazingly it was an easy decision, a no-brainer, for Dad.

I can figure out no possible way to make his sacrifices up to him other than by doing the same for my children. I hope that I've made him proud of me. I know I've disappointed him at times. But Dad also taught me independence, and that is why when I've stumbled I've always been able to pick myself up and get back into the game.

Dad was a grandfather at my age, but maybe I've waited so long to have a child because I knew I had such big shoes to fill. Like Michael Jordan's son with basketball and Wayne Gretzky's son with hockey and Jesus' son with carpentry, I am to parenthood. A few years after Mom left, when Dad added our next-door neighbor and local favorite, Ruth, to the squad it was not unlike Michael Jordan bringing Dennis Rodman to the Chicago Bulls.

I guess Dad appreciated Ruth's work ethic and rebounding potential (God knows he needed some scoring), though her game time tactics early on were unusual and politically incorrect and some eventually led to sweeping rule changes. Spanking with buggy whips and razor strops were now frowned upon. Bare-ass beatings with the same equipment could get you thrown out of the league. But eventually, Dad influenced her into shape, too. She matured into an honorable team cocaptain.

The Jack/Ruth merger included a couple of unproven newcomers (Johnny and Marla), and although I recommended a trade, Dad welcomed them with open arms. Another Dad lesson: *everybody* gets a chance to play. This all worked so well that a few years later Jack and Ruth bolstered our squad with a couple of minor leaguers (Chris and Mark), and for better or worse, this ragtag bunch was at least a fun team to watch.

Years later, after being frustrated by some blatantly obvious favoritism and painful contract negotiations ("Why doesn't Chris have to do the dishes?" "Because he is only three." "So?"), I wanted my own locker room and demanded management do away with the dreaded hair length restrictions. I exercised my options and had short stints in the Senior League (my grandparents) and a new, high-paying hair-growing renegade club with no drug policy (Mom and stepdad Number Six), but I always returned to where I belonged. Back to where my heart was. My team. Our team. Dad's team. America's team.

Daddy, It Feels Good When
I Go Like This!

Son, you're too young to have this conversation now, but you're preaching to the choir, little buddy. In certain religions and southern states, masturbating is a crime. But it is a victimless crime and should be legalized, and at a reasonably young age, too. If you're old enough to be tried as an adult, you're old enough to masturbate. Celebrities have their causes, some great (Jerry Lewis: muscular dystrophy; Bob Dole: erections), and some celebs just promote phone service and beer. I promote masturbation—self-love, baby. Why? It feels good. Admit it! And nobody can do it quite like you can. It keeps you out of trouble. As a man I have learned from talk radio that I have some sort of chemical in my brain that makes me want to reproduce every two or three seconds. But that chemical is nowhere to be found after a good *one-on-none* session in my shower (actually, I don't like to work in water; it negatively affects my grip). The point is if you travel like I do and monogamy is a must (because I love my woman and I hate condoms), jerkin' the gherkin is the answer. You can't get AIDS and you won't end up in the tabloids, unless of course you take it on the road (Pee-Wee Herman). But be warned; it's not totally safe sex. Besides the usual painful skin damage from overuse (*tug burns*), you *can* go blind beating off, if you do it in one of those tanning beds. You can't wear the goggles because you've got to keep your eyes on the door in case someone breaks in. Plus, you get a pretty weird tan. I have it down to a science, an art actually. I like lesbian porn only. I'm not homophobic. I just hate skinny guys with big dicks. Plus, you know they're all big fags anyway. I also recommend *Astro-glide* as my personal lubricant of choice. It doesn't gum up and it's water-based, so it's edible. I have no idea why that is important to me. My system is simple: (1) Get a hand towel, half-damp with warm water, half-dry for easy cleanup. (2) Pop in *Girls Who Like Girls # 69*. (3) Spread liberal amounts of "the glide" over sensitive areas. Men, don't forget the nipples. (4) If right-handed, hold remote with dry left hand. The maids know what a greasy remote means. (5) Get busy. (6) Clean up. (7) Lights out. (8) Repeat if necessary (recommended for teenagers). If all this gets boring—I don't know how it could, but if it does—sit on your hand until it goes to sleep. You get that "dead arm." Then use it. It feels like somebody else's hand.

Daddy, What Was It Like
Where You Growed Up?

Princess, it was nice. Kinda quiet, but nice. Besides the fact that a family could live pretty well in Iowa for $500 a week, the natural beauty of the state is stunning. The green rolling hills. The perfect massive orange-and-gold sunsets. You've never seen as many stars in the night sky. And then there's the animals and the streams and the lakes and, best of all, the kindest, most down-to-earth people in the world. And yet I couldn't wait to get the hell out of there.

But I do love to go back for Ragbrai, which is the *Des Moines Register's* Annual Great Bike Ride Across Iowa. Seven hot summer days on a bicycle, from one end of the state to the other. On the first day your back tire is dipped into the Missouri River, and on the last your front tire is dipped into the mighty Mississippi. Me, Mo, Mike, and my brother Mark and MacGyver are joined by 15,000 to 20,000 other riders, whose names do not begin with an *M*, from around the world in an incredible bonding experience (i.e., a drunken tit fest).

Anybody who says Iowa is boring has never been on Ragbrai. And since they've never been on Ragbrai, they've never been on a naked coed beer slide or judged a wet T-shirt contest at a Catholic church in the middle of the afternoon or ever seen pork chop or turkey leg stands set up all along the highway. When 20,000 people descend on a town of 500 for the evening, people tend to lose their inhibitions (minds). So if you are, say, a home state celebrity, you could have your hands full, literally, signing 200 to 300 bare breasts per hour. Every hour. Unless, of course, your buddy Mo takes pictures of these "meet and greets" and later mails them to you and your snoopy wife opens them up and has a shit fit. Then you are banned for life from future boob signings. Loophole: she didn't say anything about bare asses! I'm one classy dude.

When I get kicked out of show business or retire, as I'll call it, I'd love to move back to Iowa. My dream is to be governor of course (that last story probably won't help any of my future political efforts). I'd want to have a family before I ever ran for office. Not so much to celebrate with if I win, but more so to support me when I lose. Shelby, my all-time best better half, whose father was in politics, is not so thrilled with this idea: "Tom, I know you and I know you'd hate kissing all that ass." She underestimates me, but I think she'd support me if I ran (so far, she's at least promised not to vote *against* me, which is nice).

Shelby and I had the unusual privilege of being in Al and Tipper Gore's home with their family on December 13, 2000, the day Al gave up his quest for the presidency (I'd stumped for Al). I felt a little weird, like we were intruding. There were only about ten of us there and I got to see a real family at work. It was supposed to be a sad day, but the kids were cracking jokes, the wife was making food, and Dad went out and gave his little concession speech, then came back and partied until 4:00 A.M. The stiffest of the stiff actually let his hair down (he dirty-danced with Jon Bon Jovi) and had a good time! Al Gore got robbed of a nice little job with lots of sweet perks, but the next morning he'd still wake up with a wife and kids who loved him and a kitchen full of tasty treats, so I didn't feel too sorry for the man.

Mommy Likes to Eat Only This Much, but Daddy Likes to Eat a Whole Bunch!

True, boo-boo, let's just say I like to party. And since I don't drink or use drugs anymore, food is all I have left (and masturbating, but that's not very social). I eat either very good or very bad. There's no middle ground. I enjoy it. Too much, I'm told. I've got to be careful because it frightens my loved ones. I'm most comfortable indulging in the privacy of my own home, but sometimes you have to go public. For me it's always a pretty fast process. I like to get the food coming right away, and lots of it. And we're going to have dessert, probably several. Some times I sweat. I guess it's the excitement, but I hate that look that other diners get when they're shocked and disgusted by my gorging. That's why I like to hang out with my friends from Iowa. They don't judge because they're all big and we all eat big and we all sweat. Big.

A few years back my friend Chris Farley, the actor and best man in my second wedding, was in Pritkin food rehab in Santa Monica. He'd sneak over the wall in his fat-farm sweatpants and we'd go to Le Dome or Spago or some other fancy joint and eat literally twelve or thirteen desserts. We'd go wherever they had a giant wheel-around dessert cart. All the rich people in the restaurant would be sickened of course. The poor ones, too. Even Roseanne couldn't keep up with us, and that's saying something, mister.

One time Rosey and I went on a diet and as usual we got a little nuts and kept spying on each other. I'd find her with cookies and I'd take them, spit on them, and throw them in the trash (you know, for support). I could be controlling. Then she'd take them back out and eat them. She could be stubborn. And gross, God love her.

We once got offered $10 million ($9,999,900 for her, $100 for me) for some *Slim•Fast* diet commercials. All we had to do was eat their products and lose thirty pounds each. We agonized over the selling out of our good names. This was a long, long time ago. The company's products also included candy and these really tasty ice-cream bars. They were half the calories of regular tasty ice-cream bars, so of course we had to eat four times as many. Once a week a special diet doctor from UCLA would come over to weigh us. Nothing against *Slim•Fast*, but it soon became apparent that we were *gaining* weight at an alarming rate. We tried everything to lose the weight. Everything except diet and exercise. But we fooled them for a while. Did you know that on a lot of scales if you lean forward you weigh less? With the right scale you can drop thirty pounds. The whole *Slim•Fast* company was behind us 100 percent until they found out the truth. Then they dropped us like the fat turds we were. We did get to keep the broken scale and our cash advance. So instead of getting $10 million to lose thirty pounds, we got $2 million to gain twenty-five, which in my opinion is a much, much better deal.

Food and love are very similar things to me. I knew my grandmothers loved me because they fed me so much and they loved to watch me eat. I knew my stepmom hated me because she put locks on the kitchen cabinets. She said I was fat and that I ate like a hog. You aren't supposed to say that kind of crap to kids.

Especially if it's true. In our house if you were late for dinner you were SOL (Shit Outta Luck) and eating between meals was called stealing food. The punishment was pain and humiliation and maybe even a public front yard head shaving.

In my Iowa everything is an eating contest. Most restaurants have a sign with eating records. How many ounces of steak, how many hamburgers some guy ate, etc. (or gal; this is Iowa). People in Hollywood find binge eating disgusting if you don't puke afterward. Sweating's bad, but puking's good. I don't get it. All-you-can-eat buffets are a personal challenge to my manhood. It's like free food, goddammit! Who knows if I'll ever get this opportunity again as long as I live? When I worked at McDonald's if you unloaded the truck in the morning you got the three dollars an hour, plus all you could eat. So my usual breakfast consisted of four Big Macs, four Quarter Pounders with cheese, two large fries, two apple pies, a chocolate shake, and a Diet Coke. You get the picture. But it's not all bad. I once won $50,000 for my children's charity by winning an eating contest against Hulk Hogan and an even bigger wrestler named Typhoon. I ate seventeen pieces of pie in seven minutes. My secret? Once you start, don't stop. Otherwise your mind will kick in and tell you that you're full. In fact, too full. Sick even. Violently ill. Anyway, that's my secret. Spread it around.

Back to why I got together with Roseanne. There's just something special about a woman who when you bring a whole gallon of Rocky Road to bed and eat it all doesn't care. Try that with Gwyneth Paltrow.

Daddy, Is Divorce Bad for You?

Sometimes, honey. This is one of the few things the "Super Toms" and I do have in common. When I first got divorced, back in 1994, I felt like a failure. I was not only a onetime loser but also secondhand goods. Who could love me? But then I thought about it and realized that times have changed. Secondhand clothes are now called vintage and are incredibly popular. Used cars are often considered classics, and famous dead people's knickknacks are valuable collector's items. In other words, I was hot and very much in-vogue prime rib for single women on the prowl. Here are my six "you won't be sorry" reasons why a divorced man is the studdliest catch of them all.

1. His fear of another divorce inspires greater effort. Whether it's a friendly touch football game, a pie-eating contest, or marriage, one thing remains constant: Guys hate to lose. The divorced man will go to great lengths to prove to you, himself, and, in some cases, the tabloid media that he can win big, big, big on the great gridiron of matrimony. Just for fun, every so often tell him you don't think it's working out and watch him break land-

speed records as he cleans out every jewelry store in town and comes home with his tail wagging and an armful of sparkling peace offerings. *Bling, bling.*

2. His low self-esteem is your leash. Most of the trouble that men get into stems from having egos the size of Trump Tower. Your divorced man's ego, however, is flat-lining after the recent head-on collision that was his last marriage. As such, a careful application of both compliments and criticism will keep him nicely in check. Thanks to you, he'll start feeling like a decent human being once again. And thanks to you, he'll also understand that there isn't a Porsche red enough to make him attractive to college coeds. Not for long, anyway.

3. Next to the Wicked Witch of the West, you look like Snow White. Let's face it: People don't get divorced because it's the first official step toward having their ex nominated for sainthood. His ugly memories of her will make you seem like a goddess in comparison. In other words, anything you say short of, "I hate you," will give him a warm and fuzzy glow. So go ahead: don't shower for a week; gain weight. He'll think you're absolutely adorable. Then again, it might remind him of his ex.

4. His family and friends are rooting for you. First wives are always viewed suspiciously by those closest to the "prince." She's not good enough for him. What kind of mother will she be? Her sitcom isn't funny anymore. But as wife number two, three, or four you will face none of this. In fact, you will be as welcome as eight hours of sleep . . . something none of his family and friends got during his breakup with wife number one, two, or three when he discovered both malt liquor and cheap late-night phone rates at about the same time.

5. He's ready to share. After being told over and over that he hoards his feelings like a miser, he's now ready to

become an emotional philanthropist. He's a broken man, so he'll talk relationships. He'll become gushy about his feelings, and he'll tell you everything he knows. Just remember that it still may not seem like he's sharing— namely because he doesn't know very much.

6. He must love you a lot. Ever notice how readily a child who has never gotten a booster shot in the ass will let Mommy take him to the doctor's office? It's the same thing for a man who is altar-bound for the first time. Neither has any clue what awaits. But a divorced man is like a suspicious four-year-old who has already been asked to drop his drawers one time too many. Nothing will corral him into doing something he really doesn't want to do. Trust me on this. If he's marrying you, he loves you . . . a lot.

Dad, Did You Make Any Cool Friends When You Was in Hollywood?

Well, winky-dink, as a matter of fact, I did. See, when I was nine my dad gave me my first self-help book: Dale Carnegie's *How to Win Friends and Influence People*. That was a pretty harsh indictment of my prepubescent people skills, but Dad was trying to help.

Dad was right about one thing. I needed to know how to make some friends, because I sure as hell couldn't count on my family to meet all my emotional and spiritual needs, now, could I? Today I have friends from all segments of my life. I still hang with my buddies I grew up with in Iowa (Mike, Mo, Brownie, and Cox, et al), a few friends from my five years in Minneapolis (David Carr, Val, and Susie, et al), and now, of course, my Hollywood friends.

When I first moved to L.A. in 1988 everybody warned me that it was impossible to cultivate real friendships because most people were either snobby or bitter and everybody else was phony. And they were right, if your relationships are based on show business. I found this out the hard way one day in 1994 when I was divorced/fired. Although I did receive a very nice letter of support from Mr. Alan Thicke and Brad Pitt came up to me in a club. He was like, "Oh, my God, it's Tom Arnold! It's so cool to meet you, man!" Brad's a nice guy from Missouri, but he was probably just mocking me, so I punish him to this day by making a special point of saying "hi" to him every time he has the bad luck to run into me.

I'd given a lot of jobs out, but only a couple of those people covertly called me to ask how I was after Big R's and my breakup. I can't blame the others; show biz jobs are hard to come by. Sympathy, compassion, and loyalty are easy to recover. Between gigs. On your "downtime." In the meantime, I had to get some new Hollywood friends. Unfortunately, I was currently and perhaps permanently unemployed and constantly shamed in the media, so my prospects for superstar friendship were nil. I basically had one Hollywood friend/employee left, and that was my assistant, Kim. And since I no longer did anything that required assisting, I had to let her go. But she stayed loyal (kept quiet about . . . stuff), and I will always appreciate that.

Of course I screwed that up, too. We started dating. Publicly even. It went very well for a couple of weeks, until one day the phone rang in my condo and I asked her to get it and she said, "I'm not your fucking assistant anymore, remember; you fired me." Women. She didn't even mention the generous severance package she'd received, but it didn't matter because I knew that it was over. *Don't Shit Where You Eat* should be the title of this book.

Various members of my family came out from Iowa to help me with my transition from TV star to suicidal lowlife, but I had to send them packing after they wrecked all my cars. I decided I had a better shot at working through this alone before I had to start taking the bus. That's when a funny thing happened. I made some real friends.

The best thing about cleaning up your life is that you tend to attract a better class of friends. People who genuinely care about you. People who are there for you when you're down. People who welcome you into their lives. People who don't smoke crack. The kind of friends that are so decent and kind, you feel sorry for them having to be friends with you. And you spend your days and nights wondering what incredible things you could do to make it up to them.

I believe that if you're going to be happily married, you need to have friends who are happily married. Turns out the happily in happily married is a different happily than the fairy tale happily in happily ever after. It's like how we overuse the words *brilliant* (the British are the guiltiest at this) and *genius*. Nobody's brilliant all the time (Bill Gates; the man can't even drive a Harley) and everybody's a genius sometimes (even me; read my chapter on masturbation)

What I've learned is that if you go into marriage expecting anything more than loyalty, a little friendship, a dash of compassion, a pinch of respect, and a whiff of romance you will probably be pretty disappointed. Now if you can accept this and keep your expectations reasonably low, you will enjoy wedded bliss. Wedded bliss is this sorta semicoma state you have to live in 75 percent of the time so you can recharge your phasers to full strength, so when you are really needed to be a loyal romantic, compassionate, respectful friend you show up like the champion you are. It's also good to recharge because in marriage you spend a hell of a lot of time and energy defending yourself. Past, present, and future.

It may sound simplistic, but the key to a successful marriage is love. Unconditional love. The kind of unconditional love that makes a fat man thin, at least twice a week for twenty to thirty minutes at a time. The truth is, if you did not unconditionally love your mate, you would kill them because of the things they say to you. Some would call those things honesty. Some think that they are trying to help. That it's their job and their job only to let you in on the truth.

Ever notice that your wife doesn't think you are funny? Even if most everybody else does? She can't. Why is that? Because she's trying to protect you? Because she's trying to protect the public at large? Not to worry; nobody's wife thinks he is that funny. I've seen Robin Williams's wife, Marcia, a good woman, shoot him down with the look of an eye. That look that says, *Wrap it up, honey.* That look that takes the wind out of your sails. That crushes you and makes you feel small. Yes, the look of love. Unconditional love. As men, we could never do this. Our job is to build our sweetie's self-esteem. Some of us are so good at this that our partners eventually realize that they are, in fact, too good for us, that they never really needed us, and so they leave!

Steve and Jamie Tisch are my friends. They are very loving and generous, well-to-do, and down-to-earth folks. As down-to-earth as you could be with a movie theater in your home. They have a couple of dinner parties a week with the coolest assortment of folks a big kid from Iowa could ever dream of breaking bread with. Artists, designers, Madonna. You name it. Steve and Jamie are also "family." The family I've fallen into/built for myself. Steve's a nice guy, an *Academy Award*–winning producer/philanthropist and best man in mine and Shelby's wedding. Jamie's a supermodel-caliber beauty/home accessory store owner/fund-raiser and, oh yeah, mother/stepmom to five great kids with Steve (one is my godson Zach). In a perfect world, Jamie would've been my mother and Steve would've been, well, he would've been my buddy, so I guess that worked out nicely.

During my last divorce, when I was at my lowest, they forced me out of my house day after day until I was almost too embarrassed to wallow in loathing and self-pity anymore. Damn them! It's nice, because I love them both and I can count on them. I can be honest with Steve and Jamie about anything and they with me. Steve, who'd give up his Oscar for *Forrest Gump* to be a stand-up comic, and I like to gossip about our peers, and Jamie and I talk a lot about the joys of stepparenting. Jamie knows that, like in a real family, if she says that Steve's being a jerk, I will listen, sometimes agree, maybe eventually even try to help, but I will still love Steve.

If we're going to sound off about our spouses, and everybody needs to, for God's sakes—you can't live in a vacuum—we need someone we can trust. Someone you can say, "I can't stand that crazy bitch today," to and it won't affect the way they feel about her one iota. (Women hate the term *crazy bitch*, but men don't seem to mind being called *lazy prick* or anything else, for that matter; weird, huh?) Good friends get involved. I do. If there's a chance that I can make something better in my friends' lives, I go for it. One hundred percent. That's probably 80 percent too much, but that's my deal. Sometimes you annoy people, sometimes your feelings get hurt, but if my friends are involved, I'm there. If my friends' kids are in trouble, I'm there, too. Believe me, if you want your friends to really love you, help their kids sometime. This is also an excellent form of birth control.

Women friends tend to be a little kinder, more selfless, more open. Another nice thing about having women friends is that when they do complain about their man, I often find myself saying, "Oh, that's too bad," but I'm thinking, *Hey, wait a minute, I do that, too; maybe I should stop.* When I hear a buddy bitching about his wife, I listen; I tell him it sounds terrible, but I've been through worse. Then I ask him an important question: "Isn't she the mother of your children?"

My point is that if a woman bears and rears your offspring she has already done more for you than you could ever repay. And she knows it. So yeah, she's a little nutty and sure, she can occasionally be a little mean, but get over it, fucker! Besides, you like to isolate in your office and you like to ignore problems, and you have the attention span of a gerbil . . .

Since most of my friends are large men and their wives are tiny, it's also funny when the wife, concerned about her husband's weight, after suggesting, indicating, and insinuating, as a last resort, will actually try to lose the weight for her fleshy man. To set an example. To help him. Sadly, this doesn't work. He doesn't care or doesn't get the hint and she ends up anorexic, and then he can say that she can no longer gripe about his lard because now they both have eating disorders. "Who is she to talk? Crazy bi—"

Even though we are the same age, Nancy Davis is the big sister I never had. I love Nancy. She is a beautiful blonde and the most thoughtful person on the planet. Yes, even more thoughtful than *moi*. I met Nancy eleven years ago when Roseanne and I spoke at the Barbara Sinatra Child Abuse Center (they don't promote child abuse; they're actually against it). Afterward, Nancy's parents, Marvin and Barbara, hosted a dinner at their "winter cottage" in Palm Springs. Rosey and I were amazed. The table gifts at this little shindig were worth more than the art and jewelry we'd collected in our lifetimes. We thought that we were rich until that day. We felt like the Joads in *The Grapes of Wrath*. It was an amazingly opulent event in the Davises' little weekend getaway crib, a crib with a dining room that seats fifty (I'd find out later that their big house in L.A. seats two hundred and fifty comfortably for breakfast), and in the middle of this incredible extravaganza, a weekly event, I was told, was a real family. Just plain old Grandpa and Grandma, sons, daughters, and grandkids. How in the hell, I wondered, could Nancy be so normal, apart from a Ph.D. in Neiman Marcus passed down from her mother (Barbara always brags about the "World's Greatest Shopper" trophy they gave her; that's the smartest twenty-dollar investment that company ever made). After all, Nancy's house has a screening room *and* a disco.

Was it the weekly Davis family dinners? Perhaps the thirty to forty phone calls a day from her mom? Or the fact that Nancy spent a few years as a single mother raising three handsome, sometimes ornery boys, two with Aaron Spelling TV show good looks, and the youngest and funniest, Jason, has got to be the long-lost son of Chris Farley. He even played young Chris in *Beverly Hills Ninja.* Maybe the reason Nancy stays so grounded, grounded for a gal whose hardworking parents deservedly fly around the world in their own 737, is because, like her mom and sister Dana are doing with juvenile diabetes, Nancy works feverishly to cure multiple sclerosis.

Nancy does this because she cares about people and she does this because she has a vested interest. Nancy was diagnosed with MS almost eleven years ago. She complains about things like "Why doesn't the government put more money into research" and "Why doesn't Fendi give you the Gucci discount?" Yet I have never once heard her complain about her condition. So when you see the rich and famous and you wish you had what they have, be careful, because everybody's dealing with something.

In some ways it's tough to be Nancy's friend. Her gifts are always lots better than yours. Her parties are always more fun. Her thank-you notes are always prompter and better written (prompter?). And in spite of the fact that every day she shops, exercises, fund-raises, mothers, designs jewelry, lunches with ladies, and shops some more, she is always available to me by phone. Nancy's not big on the short conversations, either. Thank God for the speakerphone, or else I'd be in a neck brace. Nancy has been blessed by her second husband, Kenny. A good guy. At his birthday party Nancy toasted Kenny by calling him a flat-liner. Everybody laughed, but I knew she meant he was even-keel, a perfect addition to the extraordinary circus that is his in-laws. Shelby wishes I were more of a flat-liner. So do I, my friend; so do I.

One of my heroes, Frank Sinatra (along with the great Gregory Peck and Sidney Poitier and many others), was at that first dinner. Afterward, we all went over to Frank's place. He invited me and the other gentlemen up to his bar. No ladies allowed, yes! He talked a lot about how he couldn't possibly understand how anyone could abuse a child. He got a little misty talking about his own childhood and how he and his old friend Jilly wanted to go to Washington, D.C., during Watergate and beat the hell out of John Dean and the others for snitching. "Then we laughed when we remembered we were old men, what the hell could we do?" Frank said. Then Old Blue Eyes (you know, they were still sky blue) offered to make me a drink. I didn't have the heart to tell him I was a recovering alcoholic, figured he wouldn't understand. So I just said, "I'd love one, but the old lady won't let me," and Frank said, "No broad could ever stop me from drinking," and I said, "Well, I guess you've never been with a really big one." Frank gazed over at Roseanne, then back at me with a sky-blue-eyed look of compassion and understanding.

My first and favorite birthday.
The cake is about to be devoured!

Tommy Arnold, six months old.
Life was good.

Me, eighteen months old.
My first time behind bars.

One-and-a-half and on my way to rehab.

Me and grandma Dottie.
My body hasn't changed.

My mom at fifteen, just before
she married Dad (I don't have
any pictures of us together).

Dad, Lori, Scott, and me.
The original Arnolds.

If I would've known that in a few short years my baby sis would owe me $250,000 for legal fees, I would've dropped her.

My first car. Thirteen years later I'd be cruisin' in the hot rod in the background.

Kindergarten, 1964. I just told my first big lie.

Scott, Lori, and me. Happy children. Grandma just gave us money.

Me, poison ivy, and cousin Bucky back from "Y" camp.

Age thirteen, cute but facing years of virginity

A star by age four. From "The King and I."
Ottumwa Community Players.

Now this is a happy couple!
Grandparents Tom and Dort Graham.

Age fifteen, livin' with mom, growin'
my hair, and gettin' booze for Xmas!

Age sixteen, got a new curling iron.
Needless to say, still a virgin.

1977 Ottumwa High School graduate. One hundred sixty-five-pounds of a future meatpacker.

The Arnolds, 1974. I look like the dad, for God's sake!

Drunk, but graduated from J.C.! (with Dort and Dottie.)

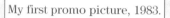
My first promo picture, 1983.

Me and Gay Chris tailing the ex in Sardinia.

"Maverick" Mike Ball and my brother Mark.

Kevin Farley, Chris Farley, and me, November 1997. This was the last time I saw the funny son of a bitch.

Me and Mo at Wrigley Field (sorry ladies, Mo has his pants on).

My beautiful goddaughter, May Moreland.

Me and Arnold Schwarzenegger. We're still friends and we're still waiting for *True Lies II*.

Jake and Dustin Hoffman and me, as a sweaty Santa in Maui. Check out the fogged-up glasses.

Me and the lovely Nancy Davis.

Me and Dad at a Hawks game.

Sister Lori, just off the bus from prison.
She should've bought a round-trip ticket.

Grandparents D. B. and Dottie Arnold. Still smiling
after sixty years (at least for the photographer).

Two fat guys and a babe. David Wells, Constance Schwartz, and me.

Michael Rosenbaum and me fishing up by Alaska. What a nightmare!

Me and Shelby, the woman of my dreams. What is she thinking?!

Jamie Tisch, Nancy Davis, Steve Tisch, me, Shelby, and Kenny Rickel in Maui at our annual holiday trip.

Santa and future Santa (Jason Davis).

Me and Shelby and a bunch of Tischs in Hawaii.

Nancy, Brandon, Shelby, Mr. Double-X Hawaiian shirt, Alexander, Melissa (Shelby's sis), and Kenny.

Me, Shelby, and my handsome godson, Zach Tisch.

Me and Chloe before she jumped off the five-story building.

World Series, 2001. My Yankees lost, but check out the picture. I won!

Melissa, Mike, Catherine, Caroline, and The Shelbster.

Me, Shelby, and Ann Marie Roos. The world's greatest mother-in-law. The night we got engaged (me and Shelby that is).

Typical glamorous Hollywood couple (dorky guy, hot chick).

GOAL!!!!!!

copyright © C.Ferré/Brian Kramer Photograph

Daddy, Why Do People Get Insanely Jealous?

There are only three reasons why people get insanely jealous, sweetheart: (1) you're cheating on them (I wasn't); (2) they've been cheated on before (she hadn't); or (3) they're humping the houseboy in your "mansion" while you're living in a trailer in a third world country (Mexico, Canada) and working your ass off on another bomb of a movie to pay the Pilates, Tae Bo, manicure, pedicure, and butt-waxing bills.

I wondered why Julie, my second wife, always acted so jealous, spying on me, checking my phone messages, opening my mail. I figured that was just one of the minor drawbacks to marrying the "young" (she was a mere twenty-one when we got together). I remembered the time I was hosting *Saturday Night Live* and Julie came down to my dressing room during a commercial break and punched me in the face because an ex-girlfriend, whom I hadn't invited—I'm not a complete moron—was in the studio audience (this particular punch did *not* help my performance). But I was honored. I thought this meant Julie really, really loved me. And she did, in 1996, but by 1999 she was over it (another drawback to marrying the "young").

Just because Julie wasn't in love with *me* anymore didn't

mean I had to stop loving *her*. So four months after our Valentine's Day breakup, I'd lost a few pounds on the *Divorce Court Diet* and was telling my trainer, Gina, that I wanted to give it another try with dear, sweet, still young, Julie. Between lat pull-downs Gina tried to talk me out of it, which I thought was strange, but I persisted. Finally she broke down crying and told me that my saint of a wife had been cheating on me for a long while with our houseboy. Yes, our houseboy! If it had been the pool boy, it would have been the perfect cliché. "Who else knows about this?" I asked.

"Everybody, everybody but you," she said.

God, was I humiliated. My assistant knew. My housekeeper. The people on my TV show. The pool boy (I bet he was humiliated, too). How the hell could they look me in the eyes on a daily basis? Come to think of it, they didn't. Young Julie also had a fling with a certain gold-medal-winning boxing champion who got his "Golden Boy" ass kicked twice soon after. Good deal. Saved me the trouble. Oh, you don't think so? The dude only weighed like 150. I've got 100 pounds on the little squirt. I would've crushed him like a grape! Popped his head like a zit! Torn his arm off and stuck it up his ass! Or not.

Brave Gina called Julie and told her that I knew the secret. Julie called me crying. She admitted everything and apologized and you know what? I felt sorry for *her* because I knew she would have to live with that guilt just as I had in past relationships. And because she was so young.

It was probably the most honest conversation we'd ever had, because I finally got to know Julie a little. I didn't like what I learned, but I no longer had to keep her on the pedestal that I'd placed her on the moment David Spade introduced me to her during his birthday party at the Viper Room. She was human and fallible and I, for once, had no guilt to bear. Later I wondered if it was my fault. Maybe I *had* been working away too much. Maybe I should never have brought her out here from Michigan, away from her parents. But screw that; I introduced her to plenty of good women she could've confided in if she was so unhappy. We went to couples counseling a lot and she was an adult (technically) with every opportunity to succeed and be happy and *she* made those choices. I believe in forgiveness (I have to or else nobody would like *me*), and if Julie would've come to me remorsefully and willing to do anything to work it out because she "loved me so damn much" I would have tried. But she couldn't bring herself to do that. Thank God she couldn't. Maybe she'll see the light as I think I have, after lots of mistakes, and become a better person. I hope so, because deep down inside I think there's a good woman.

Dad, Mommy Says You Used to Be a Big Stud, but I Think She's Teasing

What do you mean "used to be," huh? All I can say, sonny boy, is 8 million women can't be wrong. Nineteen ninety-nine was not my best year. In January, I got fired from a big-time movie, by a big-time director, after packing on forty pounds for a role. Then on Valentine's Day Julie and I were sitting in marriage counseling. As usual, I was doing all the talking and she was sitting there silently weeping. Suddenly she raised her hand. Did she finally have something to say? Why, yes, she did: "Tom, I don't love you anymore. I want a divorce, and I'm moving out."

Wow! I did not see that coming. "Happy Valentine's Day!" I snarled.

"You, too," she cooed, looking strangely euphoric.

"Can't we at least try some therapy?" I begged.

"What do you think we've been doing for four and a half years?" Good point.

It was a long and quiet ride home, if you don't count my yelling. I guess dinner and dancing was out. But no, when she got home she proceeded to get ready. Business as usual, I guess. Maybe it was PMS? I gave her a gift and when we went to bed she gave me one, too. Then good night kisses and lights out. The next morning I awoke to the sound of the shower running. I rushed in, wiped off the condensation, and by God she was still here, and *very* naked. When she saw me peeping she covered up.

"Why?" I asked.

"Because it's weird now," she says. "Don't you remember yesterday?"

And I say, "Don't *you* remember last night?"

She laughed. "Yeah, it was fun."

"I want to have more fun," I said, and she said, "Sorry, but I've got a meeting with my lawyer."

"Your what?"

"My lawyer, Tom."

"Who would that be?" I asked.

"Do you remember Roseanne's lawyer?"

Well, fuck me! I grabbed her towel to take one more quick peek and that was it, the end of the dream. No more Tom and Julie. Time to take the pictures down and throw out the Ketubah. Every four years, just like the Olympics. So after a few months of pain, suffering, and cardiovascular workouts, I was ready to find the *real* love of my life and future mother of my children. But I didn't want to repeat my mistakes.

When I met Julie, I thought she was perfect. Twenty-one, blond, and sweet. The opposite of everything I'd known. So I insisted that we immediately get engaged and then married. A couple of years later when Julie informed me she wasn't sure about the marriage (shocking, huh?) my friend Maria Shriver told me to tell her to make up her mind quick, because there was a line of women waiting around the block who'd love to be with me. I only wish I had that confidence and self-esteem, but I knew better.

Julie actually said, "It's hard to be with someone who gives so much and needs so little in return." I guess we never really got to know each other. Obviously she had no idea who I was. Needy is my middle name. Two divorces equals two strikes, but I haven't lost hope.

Then I dated a series of very nice women who, strangely, after spending "quality time" with me ran back to their exes' lovin' arms. I don't like to compete with other men. Kids are fine. I understand that a woman's children come first. I understand it, respect it, and appreciate it because that means she'll take good care of "our" kids. I've never been jealous of a child. Except one. I'd never been around a breast-feeder before. I know it's a loving, bonding thing, but this little guy was not little. He was three, had a full set of teeth, weighed over forty pounds, and was a tit-suckin' fool. He knew it bugged me, too. I figure if you're old enough to formally ask for it, you're too old to receive it. Especially from your mom. Especially in front of me. Especially since I wasn't getting any. I think he was a kid. Might've been a midget, because one time when he was refueling, I swear to God, he looked at me, winked, then gave me the finger. After that relationship ran dry, my buddies, owners of an Internet company, told me they felt sorry for me and had registered the name MarryTom.com to help me in my quest for a "soul mate." It sounded harmless, and maybe I'd get to meet a different kind of woman than I could in L.A. Might even be fun. Plus they gave me lots of stock and they were planning the IPO. Here's my diary:

December 25, 1999: Funny—I met my first date without the help of a Web site. After playing a very sweaty Santa for my Jewish friends and their children at a party last night on Maui, I met a pretty woman named Dana (pronounced "donna"). We hung out and laughed a lot. She told me that she wasn't wearing any underwear. I like her. A lot.

December 26: I took Dana and some kids to *Any Given Sunday*, the movie I was fired from (I'm a glutton for punishment). Oliver Stone, the guy who axed me, was playing my part! He even used some of my ad-libs. Unless his ex-wife has twenty-seven personalities. But I liked the movie and I considered it a compliment. Although there was one disturbing scene where the camera panned the locker room and landed for what seemed like an eternity on a huge black penis. *Penis* doesn't do that thing justice. It was a *cock!* I tried to cover Dana's eyes and the eyes of the twelve-year-old girl sitting next to me, but the damage was done. If that's the first one that little girl has seen, she's in for a lot of disappointment. So is Dana. Afterward I told Dana that I'd like to see her back in L.A., where we both lived. She said maybe.

January 12, 2000: I made it clear on the Web site that no one had to get married. But I was looking. I only had a couple of requirements. They had to be single, of childbearing age, and be willing to wear a bathing suit at the beach. They didn't have to look great. God knows I don't. They just had to have some confidence, which is very sexy. I believe it's better to be with a woman who has a big butt but thinks it's a small butt than a woman with a small butt who thinks it's big. Besides, I'm from Iowa, "the land of big butts." I mentioned the Web site on *David Letterman.* I hope I didn't look like too much of a fool.

January 13: Last night I got 75,000 hits and thousands of E-mails. Some women want to marry me; some women actually find me attractive—man, this is serious. Got lots of pictures, too. I'm proud to say I am very popular with the larger ladies.

January 15: I'm impressed by the openness and the kind comments in the letters I'm getting. Some people make fun of me. The term *loser* is popular. My best letter so far came from a gal in Arkansas: "I'm eighteen and live in a trailer. But if you marry me, you can mold me into anything you want—just get me out of the hell I live in. Thank you." No, thank *you.* Secretly, somewhere not too deep inside, if she has most of her teeth, she is my dream girl.

February 4: My buddies called and said they know a beautiful woman they want me to meet. I thought about what Dana would think. I really like her and we've been seeing each other a lot, but I figure it'll just be a casual dinner with a new friend, so what could it hurt, right? Besides, Dana thinks I'm moving too fast. This will prove her wrong.

February 5: I arrived at the restaurant to meet my new "buddy" and I was immediately petrified. My buddy, Shelby, turned out to be very pretty. Actually, very, very pretty. Also intelligent and nice, so I felt even more nervous and guilty. Shelby seemed perfect, but how the hell could I trust my own judgment anymore? Besides, what were the odds that Shelby could actually be "the one"? I was pleasant but ate quickly as usual; a short hug and I was gone. I like Dana, so I've decided never to tell her about this—after all, L.A.'s a big city; she'll never find out.

February 13: Last night Dana asked me whether I'd gone on a date. I said no. Then she said that her friend had a friend who knew a girl who said she'd gone out with me. I had no choice; I had to protect her. So I lied. And dammit if Dana didn't believe me. She said, "I know you've always been honest with me, so don't worry about it, honey." I'm an asshole, but I don't want it to be my fault the relationship ends. This fear keeps me out of a lot of serious trouble.

February 14: Today is Valentine's Day. I couldn't sleep last night, too much guilt. How I envy the sociopath. At the risk of ruining it with Dana, I went down to her office and said I lied and begged for her forgiveness. Although I know that she'll never forget this indiscretion for as long as I know her, she forgave me! Wow. That was close. I buy her a really, really nice present. I learn later on from Dana that this really nice present has set a "precedent" and that she'll be expecting monthly gifts of equal or greater value. That will teach me.

March 7: I've received 25,000 letters—a couple hundred from men, but I'm not there yet, boys. I refer these to my gay brother, Chris, who's thrilled. He tells me he is going to take his new black boyfriend back to Iowa to meet the family. He's a cute little guy and Gay Chris loves to stir things up. I'd give my left nut to be there. Dana and I are taking it slow, but I like spending time with her. She's smart and funny. My friends seem to like her, and that's important, because my friends have much better taste than I do.

March 14: I've decided to travel around the country and have some dinner dates at the end of April. Dana is not pleased. I remind her of my stock options and the fact that according to the CEO my 80,000 shares will eventually be worth $80 million! I tell her she can help me pick the women for the dates. She agrees. This could be a mistake. We argue; I explain that it's just a quick little dinner.

April 12: I've had more than 5 million hits on my Web site, and I'm ready for some dates. One of my assistants tells me I've been given all the E-mail letters—except for the ones in the "psycho file," and he doesn't think I want to read those. Wrong. Turns out the "psycho file" is for women who want to have sex with me and were kind enough to enclose intimate photos. Does that make them psycho? I think not. But it is more proof positive that I am very popular with the larger ladies.

April 15: Dana picks the dates in various cities, and the women are surprisingly decent, attractive, and interesting human beings, as far as I can tell. Is this a trick?

April 30: I flew to Dallas today and had dinner with a gal named Lindsey. She's twenty-four, shy but cute, and very nice. She had just broken up with her boyfriend yesterday! That's nice. What do you think the odds are that they'll be back together tomorrow? Pretty good, I'd say. We ate at this new Italian restaurant. The food was great. She talked about her life, and, of course, I bored her with a lot of my experiences. We said good night shortly after dinner. Nice woman. I went back to the hotel and called Dana.

May 1: Today I got to Boston and met Sharyn for dinner. Her picture made her look like Joan Jett. It was an old picture, very old, but she was cute. She told me she felt like she'd "walked into the supermarket, picked six numbers, and won the friggin' lottery." That's nice. The food was incredible, and I ordered every dessert on the menu. I knew we would be pals when she dived in like a champ. We had a fun evening, and after we parted I went back to my hotel so I could lumber into my sugar coma. Called Dana first.

May 2: I flew into Chicago and had dinner with Jura (a pretty talented wedding-dress designer from Lithuania) and her fourteen-year-old daughter, Goda. We went to my favorite restaurant, Heaven on Seven. And heaven it was. They have the best desserts (the chocolate pecan pie is killer). As we posed for our end-of-date pictures, Jura put her hand on my chest, and I realized that there was something very . . . passionate about Jura. Time to call Dana.

May 3: Seven pounds fatter and back in L.A. My work on the Web site is done. Eight million hits—not too bad, but it's a good thing I didn't buy the new Bentley coupe. Turns out my stocks were not worth $80 million or $80,000 or even $80. The company got bought out, liquidated, and everyone got fired. But I'm glad I did it. I broke my pattern of rushing into marriage and I learned a little about women—they like to tell their stories and they like for you to listen. They want to help you be a more complete man, and even if they have four kids surrounding them, they can still be lonely, and sexy.

As for Dana, in August we broke up. I think she was bored now that she didn't have that much to complain about. By the way, Shelby is now my fiancée, the very, very pretty woman I took out to dinner when Dana and I were together. I know it sounds fishy, but I swear to God, we never even talked after that night until I ran into her six months later, *after* Dana and I had split up. Maybe it was meant to be, Shelby and I. Maybe I finally met *the one*. But if not, I'll be OK, because now I know there is a line of women waiting around the block who would love to be with me.

Daddy, Talk About My Mommy, Please!

I'd be happy to, adorable. They say that good things come to those who wait. And sometimes they even come to us fools who don't. You know that you really love someone when you want them to be happy even when you are mad at them. I'm deeply in love with Shelby. Madly in love. It's a love that has grown tenfold since the first time I told her I loved her two years ago, after knowing her for only two weeks. It's a two steps forward, one step back kind of love. The one step back occurs during a crisis and then, happily, we've two-stepped out of it each and every time. It's only made us stronger.

Since this will be Shelby's first marriage and my last one, I try to be realistic. The woman is not perfect. She doesn't cook. Her glass is usually half-empty. She's always cold and she never brings a coat. She's not big on little white lies. She's gotta pretty serious fear of flying. She hates, hates, hates my cigars. She loves, loves, loves to shop, and she leaves too many lights on. Of course, because of my unconditional love, I can easily live with all of this (except the lights; there's an energy crisis, honey!).

On the positive side, Shelby is loyal, honest, stunningly beautiful, and the sexiest woman I've ever seen (she's so hot, I'd say that even if she dumped me). Shelby is smart, hardworking, funny, and close to her family. I could live without all of this except for the loyal and funny part. Her dad, Mike Roos, is a big-time political consultant and a good guy. His claim to fame, apart from a now very famous, not that much younger than him, future son-in-law, is that he's the one who first gave Ronald Reagan his jelly beans. Shelby's mom, Ann Marie, does cook and is always dropping off covered dishes or odd little knickknacks for the house. She's the best. She's a beautiful person, an eligible bachelorette, and an excellent proofreader. Shelby's sister Melissa (twenty-seven) is the classic cute "I wanna go with you guys" younger sister. She's sweet and available. Shelby also has two other younger sisters from her dad's second marriage, the adorable Caroline and Catherine. How scary it must be for Shelby, not just to be getting married, which is frightening enough for most people, but to be marrying me. And it shows occasionally.

The dream of winning Shelby's hand in marriage has been the main topic of discussion numerous times before by numerous other gentlemen. All younger than me. All nice, respectable guys. With good careers (except for the dude who called from prison). All with six-pack abs (including the dude that called from prison). Shelby would like me to point out that the dude's not an inmate, he just works at the prison, but I would like to point out that that's not nearly as funny. I was first to say, "I love you" (I had to be the first to say, "I love you" in all my relationships; I think this started with my mom) and I still constantly profess my unwavering love to Shelby. Usually because I want to reassure her, but occasionally because I want her to reassure me in return. Last night, after listing my biweekly heartfelt fifteen- or twenty-item "Why I Love You So Much and Want to Marry You, Shelby" declaration and knowing that Shelby is very honest, not one for false praise or flattery, I, feeling a little cocky, asked the tough question: "Why, honey, after you turned down all those great guys, did you decide to marry me?"

My ever so slightly insecure eyes meet her ever so beautiful blues, I'm hoping for something wonderful, and she says, "Timing. . . . Persistence. . . . You have a big heart." Whew. It took a while, but that's my girl! Once again this relationship is teaching me something new and wonderful: patience.

Shelby's wound a little tight. She worries; she obsesses. I love her for that and I can help her with it. Being older (thirteen years) I've learned many tricks to make myself happy. I have seen fire and I've seen rain. I've seen lonely days that I thought would never end. I've seen . . . (I planned to stop after the line about rain, but then I realized that I'd actually seen all that other stuff, too, plus I got a lot of pages to fill).

"Things could always be worse" is a favorite pep talk trick. Because they have been and (don't tell Shelby this) probably will be again. Life happens, dammit! I fancy myself a white trash Henry Higgins, a hillbilly Mr. Chips, if you will, so I like to teach the younguns. I tell her, "Honey, how can you be depressed about gaining four pounds when you know I'd think you were sexy even if you gained forty pounds?"

"Oh, great," she says.

"Or fifty or sixty, whatever," I say, and she's like, "It's not about you, Tom; I'm sure you'd find someone attractive if they gained one hundred and sixty pounds. You've proven that in the past."

Yes, I have, but where I come from most women eventually get pretty big, so you might as well get it over with. Besides, it's the eyes. I fell in love with Shelby's eyes, so it doesn't matter if she grows large or grows old, because when I look in her beautiful blue eyes I will always see the twenty-seven-year-old stunning hard body I first fell in love with.

But that's not the only issue I try to help her with. Money is a big one for most couples. She worries and I'll say, "Honey, how can you be down about our financial future? You've got a man who worships the ground you walk on. . . . OK, you're used to that. You've also got a great family and friends, I know that's nothing new, either, but hey, at least you and I have our health." This doesn't work that well, either, partly because it's so simplistic but also because of the fact that since I put her down as beneficiary on my life insurance policy, I'm literally worth more to Shelby dead than alive. But those old tricks do work for me. If I'm mad at Shelby I'll just pop in one of those great backyard wrestling videos and I project our lives into the action. I watch all the painful accidents and I think about Shelby and before you know it, I run to her trying once again to make things right, just grateful to God that my sweet baby didn't get severely burned by lighting herself on fire and jumping off her mom's roof at a kegger.

Sometimes when I interview guests on my TV show (*The Best Damn Sports Show Period*) and I notice in their bio that they've been married a long time to the same woman, I'll ask what their secret is. This has nothing to do with sports and I've gotten notes from the network confirming this fact, but I gotta know. "I married a good woman," is the usual response (Howie Long, Judge Mills Lane), but the governor of the great state of Minnesota, Jesse Ventura, was more precise: "Sex." (You've gotta love that guy; name one other governor that would say that on TV.)

I agree that sex, while not the only piece of the puzzle, is at least an important barometer as to how the relationship is going. If you're not having enough sex, then something is wrong. Either you don't have enough privacy, or you aren't communicating, or you're too busy, etc. And you need to work on those problems immediately so you can have more sex. For me, as a man, sex makes me feel close to my partner. Talking, listening, spending other non-naked time together is important, too, but you've gotta have sex. Otherwise, one of you (me), the one that wants to have sex more (me), gets his (mine) feelings hurt. He feels unappreciated and since he can only have sex with you and none of the other two and half billion women in the world, he gets a little frustrated. Angry even. This starts the "cycle of hurt." I've seen the cycle of hurt destroy more relationships than any other issue. It goes like this. The guy (me) gets rejected. I hear on talk radio that it's not always the guys, that there are actually women out there getting turned down by the man! I can't imagine why they would do that (gay). I may one day start a national directory of all of us rejects so we can match up. Probably save a lot of legal fees. Of course with my luck I'd get rejected by a reject. This is why hookers are popular. They're bad in so many ways, but you can kinda see the upside.

Anyway, guy gets rejected and the cycle starts. Of course, it's OK to say no: "too tired," "running late," "*Sex in the City* is on." It's bad when you get rebuffed by your beloved so that she can watch a TV show about other women having sex! But let's just say that it's a very special *Sex in the City*. Let's say it's the one where that dude who played a bad guy in the great movie *Warriors* as well as in *48 Hours* and is now dating that chick from *Mannequin* who plays the show's hobag with a heart of gold, shows his big giant horse cock. I'll understand if you're too busy, but you've got to ask for a rain check for tomorrow night.

And then you have to initiate the process (which is anything from lighting candles, running a scented bubble bath, and inviting me to join you to just shouting, "Come and get it!"). This way I could not possibly get my feelings hurt. Unless tomorrow night you say no and the next night and the next . . . Now I'm hurt. I do not feel loved or respected. Hell, you don't even feel sorry for me. And it eats at me; it doesn't make me quit begging of course, but it eats at me. What choice do I have? I can't cheat. I can't even think about cheating, because my own fantasies are rejecting me and a forty-three-year-old movie/TV star should only have to masturbate a couple times a week. Three times, tops.

Now later, when you finally give in, finally come to your

senses, finally wear down and say the magic words, "Hurry up if you wanna do it," I am at first overjoyed ("We're back!"); then suddenly and unfortunately I remember "the hurt": *How come she gets to decide when and where and if? Forget it; I don't want her pity. Am I a man or a mouse? I am a man. A horny man. Hell with it, I'm going in!* And I'm thinkin' and thinkin' and she moves the wrong way or looks at me funny and I am outta there! I'm not going to do this just to clear my pipes and her conscience. "I want to be wanted," I say. "I need to be wanted." I storm out. She thinks I'm a psycho. Now she's hurt, too: "Isn't this what he wanted?" Phase two of the cycle of hurt.

Healthy couples share their feelings. In the beginning I should've said, "What can I do to make you more interested in making love to me?" and she could've said, "I always feel so rushed. We need to spend more time together first, cuddling and kissing, you know, to warm me up." But since I didn't ask, she thought that I didn't care enough about her to spend the time to make her comfortable. She thought that I just wanted to get laid. And I of course assumed that the only way I could make her truly interested in sex with me was through years of age regression, decades of body sculpting, and massive facial restructuring.

No real man wants to cuddle with someone who finds him repulsive. And no real woman wants to just be somebody's whore. So you've got to drop everything and fix this today. Right now. Immediately. Shut off the phones, lock up the dogs, and take her hand. Pull her hair, whatever, just get in bed and stay there until everything is OK. Kathie Lee Gifford told me that's what she did to save her marriage when Frank screwed up. She weighed the pain and humiliation Frank had caused versus the family, the home, the life, and the man she knew she had, and it was simple: get in bed and work it out. Actually, God told her to do that. God is so smart. But that Kathie Lee is a good woman! Besides cohosting her old show with her when Regis was out, I've gotten to know her a little bit in real life, and when she lets her hair down she's a lot of fun. Seriously. She's different than you might expect and, get this, very sexy. That Frank is a lucky dude. When Julie and I broke up, Kathie Lee wrote me a beautiful supportive note. She also wrote one to Julie. Classy woman. Kathie Lee, that is.

Shelby has a lot of class, too. She is introspective and, like me, kind to animals, children, and old people, except she does it even when nobody's watching. She will be such a good mother. Sometimes I think about that moment when our baby is born. It just doesn't seem possible. It is just too fantastic. I think, is there anything I have ever done or could ever do to deserve that moment? Just one. Marry Shelby.

The quality of my life is so much better with Shelby in it. It's calmer, simpler, more real. Making and keeping her happy is job one for me. Shelby's biggest complaint about me is that we don't have enough quality time together. Can you imagine? This woman wants to spend more time with me? That's a high-class problem. It's not that we aren't together a lot. We are. It's just that I've been distracted even more than normal the last few months writing my memoirs. And she probably wouldn't be so peeved about our lack of face time if I'd given her more last year when I had no job. When I spent hours every day isolating in my office smoking cigars and playing solitaire. At least now I have a good excuse for isolating in my office, although strangely, every time she comes in I'm on a "break" from writing and I'm smoking cigars and playing solitaire.

As I said before I have ADHD, and I have a little trouble focusing. I imagine it's pretty frustrating to be with me. I have to focus on my TV show because we're basically live for two hours a day, and by the time I drive home through the L.A. traffic I am pretty fried. This is probably why Shelby says to me, "I only miss you when you are here." I make it a point to hug and kiss her as soon as I walk in the door at night. Then we sit down so that I can hear about her day (we do talk ten to twenty times a day on the phone, too), but I'm easily distracted. The TV, the phone, the voices in my head. And I tend to drift off.

Last week Shelby was telling me a very interesting story about how she'd gotten stuck in an elevator earlier that day. And I'm with her, playing out the scary scene in my head. Then she mentioned that there was this nineteen-year-old girl stuck in the elevator there with her and I began to drift. Shelby's story was a G-rated, against-all-odds melodrama with a happy ending while the one that I was tracking was an X-rated lesbian coming-of-age flick with a happy ending.

"Why are you smiling, Tom? I was scared."

"I'd be scared, too, honey; now what did you say that girl was wearing again?"

I am working on my attention span. Exercise and diet (no sugar or caffeine) help. But if I cannot pay unflinching attention to this woman, I should and will be institutionalized. I hate it when Shelby travels without me. Like when she and her sister went to France for two weeks last summer. Not to sound too insecure, but I asked Shelby to wear a global positioning satellite watch. Everything was OK until her cell phone died. I panicked. But I handled it as well as any man could who went sleepless and had nervous diarrhea for fourteen days. I lost twelve pounds and only part of my mind. I'm much better now, though. When Shelby flew to New York to try on wedding dresses, not to brag, but it was eight hours of sleep and solid stools 24/7.

Shelby is the most interesting woman I know. She makes a simple tale of a Sunday afternoon shopping expedition down Rodeo Drive sound like all three Ali–Fraser fights and 1980's U.S. Men's Olympic Hockey Team's Miracle on Ice narrated by Will Rogers *and* Cameron Diaz. And best yet, Shelby is the funniest woman I've ever met. Sharp, funny. Dry yet biting. And all her best stuff is directed at me. I love it. And when I rarely get upset she gives me an "easy, Ox" and all is well.

I can sometimes be one of those mixed-message jerks that

gently bitch about a woman's spending when he's the big shot who introduced her to Gucci and Armani in the first place. Shelby will say, "Don't you want me to look good for you?" But I know the truth. She doesn't dress for me. She dresses for Jamie and Nancy and the other girls. All women do this. Otherwise an edible G-string would be their uniform. Though I hate it when Shelby wears something low-cut in public. First of all, the goods are no longer on the market so why tease the consumers, and second, I've spent one too many nights filled with nervous tension, completely missing Elton John or Sting or somebody huge like that at some high-class fund-raiser, because I had to be on "nipple patrol."

Unlike a previous wife, Shelby doesn't wear the same-size shirts as me, so it's a rare honor when she wants to borrow something of mine. Like at night when we walk the dogs, she'll say, "Can I borrow a sweatshirt?"

"Of course, honey." Now I've got literally seventy-five sweatshirts in my closet, but I admire Shelby's taste so much that whatever one she puts on turns out to be the very one that I was going to wear. See, I didn't even know that I liked that sweatshirt until I saw that she did, so my subconscious told me it must be the cool one. Plus I get to watch her take it off.

Man, now that is sexy. Or like when she's naked in the bathroom and she's bent over drying her hair with a blow-dryer and then she like flips her head up. Or when she's shaving her legs in the shower or brushing her teeth or washing her hands. Or when she's just standing there. Or sleeping. Anytime, really.

Like most of my buddies, I spend my days thinking about ways to make money; and Shelby spends her days thinking of ways to spend it. Those are both hard jobs, but I'll be honest. I'd rather have mine. It's simpler. Find work. Go to work. Get paid. Come home. Shelby has to deal with the gardener, car washer, dry cleaner, dog washer, decorator, business manager, housekeeper, fish man, water man, mailman, phone man, pool man, handyman, cable guy, travel agent, tailor, florist, FedEx, messenger, mechanic, painter, plumber, party planner, and me. Still, I decided we probably didn't need a houseboy this time . . .

With a little luck, life is long, and happily ever after is a lot sweeter if you enjoy each other's company. It's easy to enjoy each other while on a vacation in Maui, but the key is to find someone you can have fun with during the six-hour flight over there. Someone you can laugh with on the ninety-minute drive to the airport. Someone you can hold hands with while you're standing in the security line. I am a lucky man. Hanks and Cruise lucky.

Dad, What's Your Funnest Job, Ever?

The "funnest"? Watch out, junior, or your mom's going to start correcting your grammar like she does Daddy's. Well, let's see. From 1988 to 1994 I worked on the number-one television show in America. Won a Golden Globe, Peabody, and Humanitas award. That was fun. After that I was in three hit movies in a row, and by 1996 I was working all the time and making $4 to $5 million a picture. That was pretty fun, too. Today I'm a cohost of a basic cable sports talk show. Who the hell did I piss off? The paying public, actually, but it's not so bad.

The Best Damn Sports Show Period is the "funnest" job I've had in a long time. And it's a good thing, too, because I needed it. In the spring of 2001, as I've said before, I spent my days sitting at home at my desk smoking cigars, playing solitaire. One day my new roommate, Shelby, on her way to work, suggested that perhaps I might try to find a job. "It might be good for you," she said. "To have a place to go. Something to do."

Needless to say, I was offended. Even though I'd only worked about six months that last three years, I was an "actor," and I explained that careers moved in cycles and the phone would start ringing off the hook again one day soon. Besides, I had *True Lies II* coming up.

"Haven't you had *True Lies II* coming up for the last five years?"

Good point, Shelby, but I wasn't going to admit it.

"You'd better do something, Tom, because I don't want to live like this."

Wow, if she's this crabby now, wait until she finds out that I am broke. When Shelby arrived home twelve hours later, I was still sitting at my desk smoking away. I explained to her that I had a job. I was writing some scripts and an outline for a book, "and besides, I have *True Lies II* coming up."

"Right, Tom, you've said that. In fact, you've said that every day to everyone since the day I met you, but you need a job to go to now, something that would require you to shower and put on clean clothes, so that your maid could maybe clean your ashtrays and fumigate your office."

That was harsh, but I forgave Shelby because she had never lived with a star before, so she obviously did not understand show business.

The closest Shelby ever came to the biz was the time she was an extra on a *Mac Davis Christmas Special*. Oh, and she has a friend who works at *E!* It's her friend's job to walk down the red carpet at awards shows and tell all the foreign actors (American ones, too) that Joan Rivers is not just some crazy broad but, in fact, a well-respected comedian—in hopes that they will stop and chat with her and her daughter so she can mispronounce their names and ask them unfortunate questions about their clothing as the cameras roll.

The next day, I was on a golf course, which is odd because I don't even golf, and my friend Lisa Jackson asked me if I'd be interested in doing a sports and comedy type talk show her friend was producing. I told Lisa that I doubted it, because something like that could destroy my acting career. Besides, I had

True Lies II coming up. But I said that I'd give the producer a call. Sometime. I called Shelby at work just to check in. I hated calling her at work because she always seemed so preoccupied with work and all. I mentioned this show. I wanted to reassure her that I was actively seeking employment.

"So did you call him?" she asked.

"Who?"

"The producer."

"Do you think I should?"

"Yes, Tom."

"What should I say?"

"Say anything, except, 'I have *True Lies II* coming up.' Phone's ringing. I gotta go." *Click.* Damn, that was rude.

So I immediately . . . smoked a cigar; then finally I dialed up show boss George Greenberg. As his phone rang, it occurred to me that if this was such a good job, why didn't my agents call me about it? But I talked to George, a nice-enough guy, and he explained the show as best he could: "It's a collision of sports and entertainment with comedy. A little like *Politically Incorrect*. A little like *Saturday Night Live* and a little like *Sports-Center*. There's nothing like it on TV now."

"No shit, George."

"Tom, why don't I call your agent [that phone call cost me $500,000] and your manager [another $500,000] and we'll get a crew together and try one out."

"I don't know if I can do that, George. I mean I've never done anything remotely like this, plus I've got *True Lie*—where do you want me?"

I came home and Shelby was pleased. The taping would be the next weekend and she wanted to go with me.

"Thanks for the support, honey."

"I'm just going to make sure you get there on time, Tom."

The taping was at a small studio on Little Santa Monica. I arrived early, well groomed and wearing exactly what Shelby had chosen. So yes, I looked like a big fat, preppy gay guy. We were greeted by Jeremiah Bosgang, another producer and probably the most excited person I'd ever met in my life. Shelby suggested that I get excited, too.

So we get into our chairs. It's me and a few ex-jocks, including Pro Football Hall of Famer Deacon Jones, a legend, and .300 lifetime hitter baseball's own former Philadelphia Phillie John Kruk. If you saw John Kruk walking down the street and had to guess his occupation, professional athlete would be several hundred choices down the list, long after garbageman, mall cop, and Burger King assistant manager. But John Kruk was a hell of a baseball player and I'd seen him be pretty funny on *David Letterman*, so things were looking up.

The shoot went well. The interplay was pretty loose and kinda fun. Especially with Kruk. I watched a couple of their preshot comedy pieces, and they weren't bad, either.

As Shelby and I walked to the car, the excitable boy producer ran up. "That was fucking great, man."

"Really?"

"Perfect. I really wanted you to do this show, but everybody else was nervous. They thought you'd be a jerk or something."

"Why would anybody say that?" I asked.

"Actually, I told them that because of a nasty incident when I was working on the *Dame Edna Show*. You and Roseanne—"

"Hold on," I said. "You can't blame me for *Tom and Roseanne*. Plain old Tom is much easier to get along with and a lot less expensive."

"Obviously. Listen, don't quote me on this [oops!], but you've got the job and we'll let you know officially in two weeks."

"Thanks, Jeremiah, but the sooner the better. See, I've got *True*—"

"Tom."

"Yes, Shelby."

"Save it."

"OK then, gotta go."

I'd taken a poll and everybody agreed (even some people that weren't getting 10 percent) that doing this show would not hurt my "acting career." In fact, my contract would allow me to do two films a year plus, of course, I have an out for *True Lies II*. I'm starting to think that I have a better shot at doing *Titanic II*. Anyway, they phoned me at the end of two weeks and asked for an extension, because they hadn't made a decision. I figured they were just waiting on Carrot Top and Pauly Shore to pass, but I said fine. Then I got "the call." I was in. Shelby was happy with me for a change. It was a good night.

Sports have always been a big part of my life. Not because I was a great athlete, although I did enjoy the competition, being a part of a team, and the free jerseys (mostly the free jerseys). Sports have always helped me get through the tough patches in life, but more often sports have provided a nice diversion to get through the boredom. When I was a kid, in the spring, summer, and fall one of the few things I could count on was legendary broadcaster Jack Buck's silky voice booming St. Louis Cardinal baseball games through my AM radio. It was comforting and it took me away from my personal little hell to baseball fields in cities I could only dream of visiting. Places where my heroes (Gibson, Banks, Rose) worked and played.

Then there were the Iowa football games with my grandpa Tom on autumn afternoons. Iowa sucked and they were terrible games but great experiences. When I was young, I coached YWCA girls softball, and I can still feel the pride I had the first time I put on my orange Union Bank Blackfoot T-shirt and the utter joy when we won the Junior League Championship. After that I helped coach the Senior League Athletics to the title. I am probably the only coach in YWCA history that celebrated victories by getting drunk with his fourteen- and fifteen-year-old players. Thank God I was only sixteen or it might have been kinda creepy.

Sports are the great equalizer of men. Even the Taliban had a soccer team. Of course, they executed the losers. Barbaric, yes, but be honest: I'm sure that's at least crossed the mind of many a Red Sox fan. Sports bond us all. Isn't that why they started the Olympics? I see people on the street and at airports and hotels that I figure I could not possibly have anything in common with, and they'll say, "How about those Hawkeyes?" or, "Cubs are looking good this year," and it's like we were lifelong friends, shooting the shit in the shower after a big game. Or at least at the urinal. Actually, let's say it's like we're at the sink, washing our hands. With most of our clothes on . . . maybe each missing a shoe, but that's it.

Anybody that says men hide their emotions has never been to the Superbowl or World Series. And we cry. We wept like babies when Cal Ripken, Jr., broke Lou Gehrig's consecutive game streak and then took a lap around Camden Yards and when Mark McGuire broke Roger Maris's home run record and his son ran out and hugged him and Big Mac picked his boy up and held him and then went and bumped chests with Sammy Sosa. Jesus, that was awesome! And what about Kirk Gibson hobbling out to the plate and hitting that homer in the 1988 World Series or Nolan Ryan's seventh no-hitter at forty-four, or Michael Jordan, seventh game of the Finals, three seconds left . . .

We started work on the show in July 2001. The week before this, I was back in my hometown, Ottumwa, Iowa, at Indian Hills Community College (Class of '81) teaching the Tom Arnold Actor's Workshop. Yes, you read that right. The *Tom Arnold* Actor's Workshop. Not a big deal in L.A., but in Southeast Iowa and some parts of Northeast Missouri I am Tom Hanks *and* Tom Cruise. I give all thirty-five students a signed copy of a different great actor's autobiography each year. Last year it was Shaquille O'Neal's. Guess whose they'll get next year? At least I won't have to suck up so much to get the books signed.

While I was back in Iowa I read some bad news in the *Ot-*

tumwa Courier. Keith Sullivan, an old buddy from the Hormel meatpacking plant, had fallen off his tractor while he was mowing a field, and darnnit if he didn't get his arms cut off. Sully, being a man amongst men, managed to gather up his limbs and start walking toward town. When a motorist in a van pulled over to offer some assistance, Sully's main concern was making sure they laid a towel down so that he didn't stain the shag carpeting with what little remained of his blood. Long story short, they flew him to the good hospital up in Iowa City, stitched his arms back on, and he was back home dreaming of hitting the tractor again so he could finish mowing his pasture. Of course, this being Iowa, forty-seven of his neighbors had already done that and everything else he needed done.

I knew that I wanted to help my old buddy from Hog Kill, too, so I grabbed a camera crew and headed for the country. This was the first work that I did for *The Best Damn Sports Show Period* and it really set the tone. I brought Sully out a six-pack of tall boys, a straw, and a couple of extra arms I pulled off a mannequin at Super Wal-Mart (complete with a farmer's tan I painted on). The interview went beautifully and I think the combination of seeing his old now-famous friend and taking several powerful pain pills really lifted Sully's spirits. Mine, too, because it was pretty damn funny!

Our show host is newcomer Chris Rose, who is a genius with the TelePrompTer; plus our open discussions are always more interesting if one guy is an uptight, conservative, goody-two-shoes mama's boy. He reminds me of my gay brother, Chris. Except Gay Chris doesn't put highlights in *his* hair. I love Chris Rose and we mix it up on the show once in a while, but he's got to work on his comebacks. "Thank you, Mr. Roseanne Barr" is so 1992.

Next we have John "Spider" Salley. A four-time NBA champion, Salley is great for the show because he knows everybody and a little bit about a lot of things. Like me, he still needs to sharpen his interviewing skills, as he tends to ask a question, then answer it himself, then ask another question in the same long, long sentence. It can be very confusing, but we're on for two hours a day, so we got a lot of time to fill.

Then there's D'Marco Farr, who was fresh from retiring from the 2000 World Champion St. Louis Rams. We tried out a lot of good people, but I liked D'Marco's youthful innocence. Every show needs a guy that's ignorant enough to think professional athletes should play the game for the joy of it and not the money. Plus, I get to make fun of his big, giant man-ass.

Michael Irvin is the only former superstar on the show. A perennial All-Pro receiver and three-time world champion Dallas Cowboy, Michael has also been arrested almost as much as I have. Thankfully, he found God and miraculously he's still fun to be around.

John Kruk, a fat, uneducated hillbilly from West Virginia, could be my identical twin brother (except I'm from Iowa). Last fall, Kruk (the ringer on our Entertainment League softball team) and I had a bet on the show: who could be the first to lose twenty-five pounds. The winner would then be considered only "grossly overweight." The loser had to walk down Rodeo Drive in Beverly Hills at lunchtime in his underwear. I had to win this bet. The horror of me, shirtless, walking amongst the rich and powerful was too much to bear. I'd had that recurring nightmare as a kid, and that was before I had a tractor-sized spare tire and tattoo removal scars. Kruk and I were weighed in every Friday, and we'd each lost sixteen pounds after the first two weeks.

Then, I saw a look in Kruk's eyes that disturbed me. Not the look of strain I usually see on the show as he's trying to think of adjectives, adverbs, verbs, and nouns to replace his favorite words, *fuck, fuckin', fucker,* so that we don't have to reshoot his segments. This was the look of steely determination of an iron man with an iron gut who wanted to get this competition over with so he could dive face-first into the buffet at the Outback Steakhouse. I was scared and I did my best to drop the last nine. Kruk did better. He did not eat anything—nothing, nada—for the last five days. He was worthless on the show, just sat there, eyes bloodshot, God knows what he was on, idling like a top-fuel funny car waiting for the light to turn green.

Needless to say, he won. He lost twenty-six pounds in three weeks and me only nineteen. Now I had to face the music, because real men honor their bets no matter how humiliating they are for them or their fiancées. Of course this would all be captured on film. Now I really felt sorry for Sully. But at least he never had his dignity amputated.

9/11 pushed the walk back a few weeks. I figured that America had suffered enough. This also gave me the time I needed to gain all the weight back and more. Actually, I probably looked better now. There's nothing uglier than a half-inflated Michelin. After thinking about Demi Moore naked (I do that sometimes, she is so hot) with a body-painted suit on the cover of *Vanity Fair*, I came up with the idea of having slenderizing black vertical strips painted down my torso.

The big day came and Shelby, her mom, and sister Melissa showed up for support. They wanted to be there. "To see history," Shelby said, "like when the *Hindenburg* exploded." Kruk, microphone in hand, waddled alongside me, mocking and drawing attention to my plight. It was a warm day, so my stripes melted and instead of a sleek basketball referee, I looked like your typical shirtless, dirty, crazy guy. If I'd been back in Iowa, I could've blended right in.

The first reviews for *The Best Damn Sports Show Period* were simple and to the point. They just substituted *worst* for *best*. My favorite was the one from that grouchy old fart Howard Rosenberg from the *L.A. Times*. He said if they catch Osama bin Laden and they really want to torture him they'll make him watch our show over and over. Awe-some!!!

Our network, *Fox Sports Net*, was thought up by two guys

sitting in a pub. One of those guys, David Hill (president of Fox Sports), is an Australian. David noticed that America is the only country in the world that has huge fan support for college athletics. So he got Rupert Murdoch to buy up a bunch of regional television stations, each one supporting the sports teams, both college and pro, in their area. *FSN* is in about 100 million homes, and *The Best Damn Sports Show Period* is the glue that holds this mighty network together. That's the way I see it, anyway.

I love working for a guy that thinks up his best ideas in a pub. I've worked for other network presidents before, and this is the first time I've ever heard of one going to a pub *or* thinking up best ideas. David Hill is one of those old-school, honest, if he thinks you suck, he'll tell you you suck kinda bosses. That is why I try to avoid him at all costs. Believe me, the man let John Madden go; he ain't gonna be afraid to pull the trigger on me.

I love doing the show because it gives me an open forum to show America my humor (dick, gay, and fat jokes). I also have the opportunity to spend a little time with the greatest athletes in pro sports. The biggest surprise for me is the guys that the media has labeled as troubled. Guys like Nolan Ryan, Ray Lewis, Bobby Knight, et al, are actually intelligent, well-spoken, decent, if misunderstood, men. Men who played the game or coached the game the way we want it to be played or coached: to win.

I hear a lot of people complaining about salaries in sports, but trust me, after you've seen a bunch of thirty-to-thirty-five-year-old guys (with families to support) who can barely walk, facing a lifetime of surgery because of hits taken playing a game that we all loved watching, you understand just some of the sacrifices these modern-day warriors have made.

So I am going to enjoy this job for as long as they'll have me (until contract time; then I'll have to play tough, of course). As "the Voice of the Fan" I don't have to be an expert on sports (thank God), but I gotta pay attention. And I've got to get better at putting faces with names. At last year's Superbowl, I, like everybody else outside of Boston, thought that the St. Louis Rams would crush the New England Patriots. I had to go down on the field after the game and interview the winners. So I memorized the Rams' lineup. Then, about halfway through the fourth quarter, it suddenly dawned on me that perhaps it was time to grab a program and familiarize myself with the Patriots, since they were the ones doing the ass kicking.

Remember, though, there are fifty-two guys on the squad and they wear helmets and everything, so I panicked. Our producer told me not to worry, he knew the names, and he'd whisper them to me as they passed by. I felt like Bob Hope ("That's President Truman, Bob"). This was important. My first time as a "real journalist." Covering the biggest sporting event in the world. I could not screw up.

So when our producer whispered, "Otis Smith," I whipped around and stuck my microphone in the face of the first big black guy I saw and yelled, "Otis, how does it feel?" (Great question, huh?)

He stopped, looked at me, and screamed, "I'm not Otis, dammit, I'm Bobby Hamilton, and I was just on your friggin' show last week, dumbass!" Bobby shoved me out of the way and the throng of real reporters gave me looks of both disgust and pity; then they nearly trampled me trying to catch a sound bite from Tom Brady or David Patten (see, I do know a couple).

One reporter remained. He stuck out his hand, finally a little support from a fellow broadcaster. "Don't worry about it, Tom."

"Thanks, man," I said.

"By the way, when are you gonna make *True Lies II*?"

Daddy, Do You Remember the Time When You Made Mommy Marry You?

Of course I do, little man. On August 10, 2001, Shelby and I got engaged. I'd asked her to marry me twice before. Once on Valentine's Day. We'd been together for only five months. I took her for a romantic weekend to the Bel Air Hotel. During dinner, I reached into my pocket and was about to pull out the most beautiful (biggest) ring I'd ever bought when Shelby leaned over and said, "Oh, my God, I've got to tell you something. I know it sounds stupid, but I'm sick to my stomach because I thought, get this, that you were going to propose! Crazy, huh?"

"Insane," I said as I stuffed the ring into my sock.

Later that night I admitted my intentions. Shelby cried not tears of joy but tears of pity. Hell, I'll take that. Needless to say, it was a mercy-filled night of lovin'.

I tried again exactly ninety days later (she told me not to ask again for at least three months) during a heated argument: "If I didn't care about you I wouldn't do this: *Will you marry me???*" Surprisingly, Shelby again passed on my offer of a lifetime of bliss.

But August 10th would be different. We'd been together for

about eleven months, lived together for six, and were success-
fully parenting two very troubled but lovable dogs.

I wanted this proposal to be different, which wasn't going to
be easy since I'd already proposed twice to Shelby and God
knows how many times to others (six, I think; not so bad when
you consider I started this quest when I was eighteen). How
could I impress Shelby? What could I do that would blow her
mind? It had to be special, a moment in time that would bond
our two souls for eternity. It had to be romantic and intimate.
It had to be on national television.

I open my show with a usually quick, sometimes humorous
story about my day. But Friday August 10, 2001, would be different. Without notifying anyone, I looked into the camera and
said, "You know, I love sports and I love doing this show, but
the most important thing in my life is my relationship with my
girlfriend, Shelby. She's the reason I wake up in the morning,
usually because her alarm goes off so damn early. Every night
we have dinner in front of the TV and watch this show; as a
matter of fact, we're doing it now. Hi, honey! I love you very
much and [I pulled out a new Flintstones-size ring; with each
proposal the diamond got bigger] I want to spend the rest of my
life with you. Will you marry me?"

After work, I dashed home and as we were getting ready to
go out for dinner I suggested we watch the beginning of my
show on the satellite. As Shelby watched me propose to the
camera, I pulled the ring out, got on my knee, and joined in with
myself: "Will you marry me?" She said yes! We hugged. A little
smooch. I was so very relieved (and happy).

We went out to celebrate and Shelby's mom, Ann Marie, and
sister Melissa joined us. I'm lucky that Shelby's so close to her
family because I know that she'll never get lost in all of my
hubbub. In the spirit of the momentous occasion, after dinner I
made a rare appearance at an L.A. nightclub. Shelby, sister in
tow, was enjoying herself in spite of the hubbub around me. As

the fifth person approached and asked for an autograph I, being the people-pleasing fan favorite I am, looked the woman in the eye and said, "Sure. Have you got something to sign?" She just stood there frozen, in awe I guess (maybe it was the pulsating French techno-metal), so I stated, louder this time, "I'd be happy to sign something, but I don't have any paper!"

She didn't flinch, just stared, and I noticed that her eyes were tearing up when I realized she looked kinda familiar. Then it hit me; it was Julie, my most recent ex-wife! She looked different, longer hair maybe, lost some weight. "I leaned out," she said. Then the panic set in. Would Shelby, who's next to me talking to her sister, flip out?

More important, would Shelby be mad at me, somehow blaming me for this freakish coincidence, throwing the ring in my face, and streaking out of the club, never to be seen again? So I blurted out, "Julie, sorry I didn't recognize you. Shelby and I got engaged tonight. Shelby, Julie. Have you guys met? What a coincidence, huh, girls?" Julie drifted away, and thank God Shelby was not too freaked out. We left immediately, but Melissa's friends stayed so they could critique Julie's dancing, drinking, wardrobe, and hair. Women.

As I whisked Shelby to the car, I promised that the odds of us bumping into Julie ever again in a big city like L.A. were zilch. I hadn't seen Roseanne, except for a brief nonverbal encounter at the Playboy Mansion, in eight years. So, of course, we ran into Julie the very next night at the Madonna concert. But apart from a quick call Julie made to me on 9/11 (I even felt guilty about that) we haven't spoken. I tend to feel sorry for people like Julie, and Shelby tends to remind me that I shouldn't. Shelby's good that way. Keeps me out of trouble.

The producers of my show took a poll on the Internet and most people thought Shelby would say no to my proposal, but if she did say yes, they wanted me to bring her to the studio to appear on Monday's episode. In retrospect, knowing that Shelby was such a private person and knowing the damage that public pronouncements of love and displays of affection had done to a certain previous relationship or two, I may have been pushing things, as usual.

Shelby begrudgingly agreed to show up on Monday, as long as she didn't have to be "on camera." All was well until one of my partners thrust a mike in her face and asked, "What do you love about Tom?"

She gave off such an icy stare that the stunned director yelled, "Cut! Let's rethink this!"

On the way home I tried to freeze her out. I just kept thinking, *How could she do this to me?* On national TV, on my show, I was humiliated!

Since she didn't get that I was giving her the silent treatment, I was forced to tell her I was (which kind of spoils it). She informed me again that she's not a public person and that she believes that certain moments in one's lives should be romantic and intimate. Even though I knew that before, this time I really got it. I promised to respect her boundaries and conduct myself differently in the future (although, ironically, I am writing all this in a book).

Daddy, Were You Born That One Time When 9/11 Happened?

Yes, I was, precious, and I'll never forget it. Tuesday, September 11, 2001, started like any other day. I'm awakened at 7:20 A.M. by the downstairs kitchen phone ringing. I cursed myself for forgetting to turn off the ringer. I look at caller ID; it's Shelby's sister Melissa. I let it go to voice mail. I page the maid and have her quiet that phone. Melissa immediately calls back, as she always does. I ignore her as I always do, but she persists and I answer her sixth attempt (she usually stops at three): "What!"

"Turn on the TV; terrorists have attacked the World Trade Center and it's all gone!"

"What? Shelby, wake up!"

"Oh, my God."

We watched the replay over and over. That moment I knew that my life would be different, not as safe, not as exciting, not as fun. Like when the doctor says, "I've got some really bad news." I was stunned but shed no tears; Shelby cried and cried. Her mom and sister came over to cry and watch the horror with us, but I was strong. He-man strong.

After a few hours I decided that the world was not coming to a complete end and gave up my initial notion of getting lots and

217

lots of drugs. So we ordered lots and lots of food. The cheese steaks and carrot cakes comforted me while I comforted the women. That's my job; I'm a man. I thought about the victims and their loved ones and I selfishly thought about me and my new sports-and-comedy show. Would there ever be sports again? Would there ever be comedy?

But I was tough, for the ladies. They cried some more and I searched for and reported nuggets of good news: "My friend Steve's all right!" "They found another guy alive." "Guiliani says it's going to be OK; so does Larry King." I needed things to be OK. I decided that Shelby could not be sad or afraid. I had to be fine so others could be fine. Since I was four and my mother walked out I knew that there would be days when the world came crashing down, but I also knew that life would go on, and maybe even better than it would've been.

Thursday I went back to work, because I'm a man and that's what we do. My quest for comfort from my routine was again shaken when I learned that one of our cameramen, Thomas Pecorelli, was aboard the first plane that hit the towers. He left behind a pregnant wife. People were crying, so I tried to comfort them, to get them to laugh. They had to laugh, I insisted; it was the American way.

Saturday was the Shaqtacular. An event put on by my neighbor Shaquille O'Neal, the most dominating presence in all of sports, to benefit at-risk kids. Although everything else in town was canceled, Shaq didn't want to disappoint hundreds of children, some for which 9/11 was *not* the worst day of their lives. Shelby, Melissa, and I went and Shaq and I and a few other celebrities entertained the kids. Things were looking up.

Afterward, Shelby took our dogs, Chloe (shihtzu) and Charley (Maltese, although Shelby believes he's actually a poodle mix, but he can't be a poodle mix because I would never have a poodle), to a barbecue on the roof of a friend's apartment and I went home to watch *CNN*. An hour later, the phone rang and it was Melissa; because of the state of emergency I answered immediately. She was crying hysterically, "Oh, my God, Chloe died, she fell off the fifth floor roof, and Shelby is inconsolable!"

"What? Let me talk to Shelby," I demanded. I could hear the other partygoers weeping and yelling.

"She can't talk."

"OK," I said. "Get the dog and bring her and Shelby home so I can make everything all right again."

Finally, I got Shelby to talk. She was devastated. Her friend had told her that dogs were on the roof all the time and they didn't need to be leashed. I wanted to kill her friend. You don't know how much you love a stinky little dog until she plunges to her death from a Hollywood apartment building. "Bring Chloe home, honey, and we'll bury her in the backyard and get a cute headstone with her face on it, then we'll go buy another dog, and everything will be OK; I promise. I love you so much and it's not your fault baby." It might have been a little her fault— the dog should've been leashed—but these kinds of mistakes are good practice for having kids. I'm just glad it wasn't my fault. I don't know if it was Shelby's grief or the little critter's death or 9/11 or everything, but I began to wail, "No, no, goddammit. Poor little dog, poor Shelby, why?" I pounded the bed and cried hard. Maybe harder than I ever have, because I knew that things were *not* going to be OK this time. Ever. I knew that I would not get married, much less have kids, because Shelby would leave me, and I knew that my career was over because I could never be funny after all this goddamned sadness. I realized that everything I'd ever dreamed about and worked for was gone! No more TV, no more movies, no more love. I sobbed like a little girl, or at least a four-year-old boy.

Then the phone rang. It was Melissa. Turns out that when Chloe fell off the building, the girl that lived there immediately ran downstairs and found the dog, and even though her fall was only broken by an iron barbecue, Chloe was lying on the sidewalk alive! Barely alive but still alive, and she was on her way to the hospital. "Thank God! It's a fucking miracle!" I called Shelby, who'd walked down to the point of impact, and she was weeping extra hard because she couldn't even find Chloe's body. "Honey, Chloe's alive and on the way to the hospital and whatever it costs, we'll fix her! I promise!" I felt heroic, though I'd done nothing, and was grateful because even if Chloe died, it wouldn't be as painful as when she had died ten minutes ago. Kinda like the old joke about the guy that's house-sitting and calls his brother and says, "Your cat died," and his brother's like, "Jesus, Frank, can't you break it to me more gently?" "How?" "Well, call and say the cat got out of the house. Then the next day call and say the cat's on the roof. Then the next day . . ." The brother apologized and a couple days later he calls again: "Hey, Frank, Mom's on the roof."

So I sprint to the car and am about to race to the hospital crossing my fingers, praying, desperately making deals with God (no more cigars). As I pull out, I realize that I haven't thought of everything. So as not to jinx anything, I whip back in and run up to my closet and put on my lucky red shirt. I will take no chances. This is the shirt I was wearing when I coerced Shelby into marrying me.

During the twelve minute drive I fantasized about Chloe pulling through and Shelby being overjoyed and happy, maybe even horny, what the hell. I also remembered that only two months before, fearing she was untrainable, I'd given Chloe away to the housekeeper. The dog was almost out the door when Shelby put her foot down. For my sake, I hope Shelby has blanked this memory out.

It's quiet at the hospital: "Hi, I'm Tom Arnold and I'm here about my dog Chloe Arnold." They can't find her. "What!" Soon I realize I'm at the wrong hospital. (There are two animal hospitals within 100 feet of each other in Studio City, California; that's crazy, man). Anyway, I see Shelby and some of the former revelers and immediately rush in to help. Chloe (Roos, not Arnold—I changed that immediately), with barely a faint pulse, had a broken pelvis, missing teeth, and several other things that needed fixing. "Money is no object, Doc," I say.

"That's good, Tom, because it's going to cost about forty-five hundred dollars." "Say what?"

"It's also a big risk, Tom, because odds are she'll die anyway."

It was decision time. All work stopped, and everybody looked at me. At this point I tried not to think about the $10,000 I'd already spent on this sickly, injury-prone, hard-to-train mutt in the last year.

"Do your best, Doc," I said and a team of specialists and machines converged on crooked little Chloe.

Shelby was grateful but asked, "I thought you hated the dog?"

"Why would you think that, honey?"

"Because that's what you always said."

"I was kidding, baby. I love that dog." And I did, but all I could think was, *Boy, now this better get me laid.*

Soon, I was coming around and so was Chloe. After a couple of days of touch and go, Chloe pulled through, bless her little bruised heart. So of course, I kept my end of the bargain with the Lord and gave up cigars, for forty-eight long hours. See, I want to control my destiny, my bad news. I don't like surprises.

Daddy, Mommy Says You're Not Very Good with Money and If It Wasn't for Her, We'd Be Living in the Whorehouse

I wish, bubba-lou. Actually, we'd be living in the *poorhouse*. Besides, it's a sin to die a wealthy man. Andrew Carnegie said that; of course he was loaded at the time. Going broke when you're young is kinda fun. You scrape all your pennies together, cash in a few bottles and cans, and buy a six-pack of Pabst Blue Ribbon. You've got your priorities. Who needs toilet paper when you've still got coffee filters?

Growing up, I never felt poor; we just didn't have any money.

In my early twenties, when I moved from Iowa to Minneapolis to become the comedy star I am today, I was broke, but so were my roommates, and at least we all had our own couches and bongs. No peer pressure here, just a few comedians, a liquor store clerk, and a thirty-five-year-old paperboy. We called our house the Bohemia Club. It was fun, but looking back, I wouldn't let my stinky-assed dogs live there. Some of us actually had cute girlfriends who spent time in that dump. Try getting that in L.A.

Going broke when you're forty-two is a scary, embarrassing, and surprisingly liberating experience. I used to go broke a lot, but once I got off cocaine going broke seemed, thankfully, out of my reach. Then last fall, after thirteen years of unflinching relative financial security, my bottom line bottomed out.

If you watch *Entertainment Tonight*, you are probably shocked. How could a guy who got $50 million from Roseanne ever run out of money? First off, let me get the record straight. As good a story as that is (and I hate to ruin a good story), the facts are much less newsworthy. When Roseanne and I split I got zero alimony. A judge offered me a minimum of $100,000 a month, and because of pride and stupidity, which often go hand in hand, I said no. That alimony money is good stuff, because that shit is tax-free! Second, our divorce settlement, which involved potentially a couple hundred million dollars (we had no prenup and *Roseanne* was syndicating), was simple. We owned two houses side by side in Brentwood (we weren't really getting along). We figured the value of said properties and I took half. About $5 million. Now $5 million is a lot of money, but I also was a workingman (three TV series, some movies, including *True Lies*) and had made well over that. But, the bottom line was that because of *True Lies* I had other movie offers on the table and I didn't want to go to trial and plead poverty. Although it might have been interesting, because Roseanne would've had to say that I was talented and had a long and successful career ahead of me. That would've been fun. Truth is, because California is a community property state I passed on $30 to $50 million. And she still hates me!

So I felt pretty good about myself. At least I did until the fall of 2001. My advice to young people coming into money is simple. Pay attention, sign your own checks, and watch out for the red flags. Like if your accountant suddenly gets new offices or his son is your lawyer or his father is your financial adviser, stuff like that. Don't completely trust anyone. But being the jackass that I am, I didn't pay enough attention and for seven years I trusted one man who signed his own checks.

Shelby, whose greatest professional attribute is that she's a nit-picking wench (detail-oriented perfectionist, as she likes to say), started paying attention. Details are boring, but the bottom line is I was paying like ten times the going rate for, in my humble opinion, not super-competent work and, idiot that I am, didn't notice because I thought we were friends. My bad.

When the shit hit the fan it appeared, for a few days, that I had no money left. In fact, I owed a million or so. M. C. Hammer time! This from a guy (me) who's made $25 to $30 million over the years (not Cruiseville but nice). Sounds like a lot, but 45 percent to taxes, 10 percent to manager, 10 percent to agent, 5 percent to business manager, and 5 percent to lawyer. You take out publicists, lawsuits, massages, and cigars and you see the problem. It didn't help that I was a millionaire living like a billionaire. One day, I looked at my neighbors' houses. The one behind mine is a multibillionaire's and the one in front is Shaq's, so I'm thinking, *All these dudes are really, really rich and I'm, well, Tom Arnold. I should probably move.* My divorce settlement to my second wife was costly, too. I would've saved money there if someone, anyone, had been able to be more honest about my total lack of finances.

Anyway, during my three or four days of hard-core bankruptcy I learned a few things. I learned that something deep inside of me has always expected to be in this position and that I needed to straighten that out or I'd never completely get out of this mess. I learned that material things mean little to me (it's the fame and money itself that's important). I learned that I have some very good friends, who offered support of all kinds. I learned that I had to change my lifestyle, and, most important, for the first time in years I knew beyond a shadow of a doubt that somebody was loving me for something other than money. Although I don't doubt that Shelby had at least a little "crush" on the cash. So did I, quite frankly. So did I.

I think others cared for me, but when you're older, balder, and fatter than them you always wonder. But Shelby was a trooper. I waited for that moment, that "well, I'm outta here" moment that I'd had with every other woman in my life since day one, but it did not come. And I pushed and prodded and poked trying to open up that dark place that I knew was in all women, that place that spewed the "Did you seriously think I was actually in love with *you*?" bile.

I knew just as sure as the sun went down every night that this would happen. That my game was over. My mom left when I was four and I've never had a relationship with any woman make it to five years. So I waited. And waited (it seemed like an eternity, but it was only a couple of days). But it just didn't happen. Talk about your nice surprises. Talk about feeling loved. I was glad I went broke because now I was sure. But since I was sure, it was time to take that for granted and start obsessing about the financial hell I was in. With Shelby (a little tattered, a little torn) by my side, we got back to business. The next week we located some hidden cash and we were back to zero. Then we found a little more and we didn't have to move. Not today, anyway. But I gotta give up the Cuban cigars. Too expensive, plus now I really owe Shelby and I need to live awhile to make it up to her. I told her that the good news is she didn't have to worry about signing a prenup. And she's like, "A prenup for what?" I have a feeling I'm going to be hearing about my financial incompetence ("How could you not know these things?") for many fun-filled years to come. If I'm lucky.

Dad, What Are Women Really, Truly Like?

That's a good question, chief. Well, they smell good and they're soft and sensitive and nurturing, but most of all women are . . . unpredictable. For instance, Thursday afternoon, my dressing room phone rings. It's Shelby. She's crying. "What's wrong honey?" I ask, and she sobs, "I'm sorry I put so much pressure on you, Tom. I know I spend too much money and I appreciate how generous you are and how hard you work. I don't want to make you have a heart attack."

Wow, that felt good. Real good. My spine was tingling like when my grandpa sat beside me and helped me skin squirrels as a kid. I felt the love, too. The lump in my throat took me back thirty years, to the day Dad came to the Y so that I wouldn't get my ass kicked again by these three local toughs. They ran when they saw him. He yelled, "Chickenshits!" That was a good day. So was this. I was loved. I was appreciated. Maybe even respected.

I told Shelby, "Don't cry, honey. You don't spend too much" (lie). "It's my fault; I encourage it" (fifty-fifty). "You do so much for me that you more than make up for it" (truth). "Besides, I love working, night and day, for our future, hell, our kids' fu-

227

ture." She calmed down and when I hung up I was shaking. I'd been blindsided. I'm not used to being apologized to, much less an apology/appreciation combo. At that moment, I felt as good about myself as a man with 27 percent body fat can.

Dad, Are You Saying That All Women Are Crazy?

In a word, yes. But if you tell your mom I said that, I'll deny it. If you're looking for one that's not crazy, Son, stop; you're wasting your time. My mothers, grandmothers, exes, costars, sisters, Mother Teresa, all are crazy . . . sometimes, and that's the key. The good ones are crazy 2 percent of the time and the bad ones 80 percent or 90 percent (anyone over 90 percent is usually locked up or starring in a sitcom). Being with a good woman is like driving a great car with an occasional catastrophic fuel ignition problem. It's usually a comfortable, smooth ride, but the car will suddenly explode and burst into flames every 1,000 miles or so. But that's the chance you have to take, because you don't want to be one of those guys who have to walk to work.

Shelby often wonders (aloud) why we're together if we have so little in common. She loves to talk about our sissy dogs, shoes, purses, and jewelry and I like to talk about sports and current events. My theory is that if she read the front page of the paper once in a while, she might forget about those Jimmy Choo boots. Her theory is that if I could fit into normal-sized clothes, I'd give a serious shit about fashion. This is why I encourage her to have gay male friends and why she encourages me to do the same.

It's Friday and I'm still basking in the glow of mine and Shelby's Thursday afternoon telephonic love fest. Little did I know that the car was about to explode. We meet after work for dinner with eight or ten of my coworkers. She arrives late saying, "I don't know why I'm here; this looks like a work meeting."

I try to calm her by saying, "No, honey, it's casual."

She fires back saying, "I suppose you're paying for everyone," to which I proudly respond, "No way, baby; the boss is buying." Checkmate, right? Not even close.

I ask Shelby if she happened to get my message about my plans for the next day. I asked if I could skip her little sister Catherine's ninth-birthday horseback-riding adventure so that I could work on my soon-to-be-long-overdue book. I figured that this would be fine since Catherine and Shelby's other little sister, Caroline (ten), were coming over after the ride to stay with us and we'd all have good quality time then. Besides, I figured, I'm severely allergic to horses.

Shelby was incensed. I don't even know why I bother to figure anything anymore. "We always do stuff with your friends. My family likes you, Tom; don't ruin it."

Who is this evil woman who won't give me a break? I was furious, and we carried on a low-talking argument in front of my peers. ("I'm just gonna leave," "No, *I'm* gonna leave.") Until dessert came and distracted me. Didn't she understand the pressure of being a movie/TV star and a big-time book writer? What happened to Thursday's Shelby? I want her back. Friday Shelby sucks! My mistake, as always, was trying to use logic. Logic has no place in a relationship with a woman. Maybe I do need more gay male friends.

So pouting Thomas woke up Saturday, took a handful of horse pills, and we drove to Malibu. Only my horse would suffer more than me on this day. The medication's 1 percent chance of drowsiness and general feeling of quaalude/acid trip side effects had kicked in as we rode (actually, *rode* sounds too fast; we more or less hobbled) around a beautiful junkyard overlooking Charlie Sheen's mothballed bachelor pad for an hour. This wouldn't have been so bad, but Pecos Pete's "Safety Speech" took two.

On the way home, Shelby was happy again and said I could go to my office and write away until the little girls got there. Which gave me exactly three hours to watch auto racing, stare out my window, smoke cigars, and hallucinate.

Mom Says All Men Are Stupid. Are You Stupid, Dad?

Oh, yeah, precious, we all are. In the same measure that women are crazy, men are stupid. Women, I think, misinterpret this stupidity for meanness, and that gives them a license to kill. Where is the compassion for the jackass? I can honestly say that I have never said anything mean-spirited that was intended to put a woman that I loved down. It just sounds that way sometimes. But because of the knowledge gained through my past failures and thirteen years of couple's counseling I know that, "Because I pay for everything," is not a fair response to the question of why I believe I put more than my share into the relationship. Or any other question, for that matter.

It seems to me that serious relationships are very competitive. Everything has to be even and "because I pay for everything" is a plus mark in my column, but it is one better left unspoken and never ever yelled. I consider Shelby and me even. I give myself a 6 in the looks department and I'm supernice (just ask my friends) and, for a man's man, I'm pretty frickin' sensitive. I give lots of compliments and if she says, "How do I look?" I assume she wants to hear something nice.

Shelby, on the other hand, is very honest, which is a positive, I know, but when I ask her how I look, she actually looks at me and gives me the unkind truth. So for niceness I get a 10, and that gives me 16 points. Shelby's a 10 for looks, of course, and an 8 for nice. That's 18 for Shelby, but I deduct 2 points for her taste in men and we are all tied up.

I'm not really worried that Shelby thinks besides our love we have so little in common. I think that's just the nature of the man/woman relationship. It's more important that we try to meet each other's needs. Now that's not always possible, but it's the trying that's the most important. Otherwise, she'd marry an independently wealthy, shopaholic, gay guy horse whisperer who likes to cuddle and I'd marry a bisexual, agoraphobic pastry chef hooker with an outside jump shot.

Things I *Want* from My Wife

Before my first marriage I didn't know anything. Before my second marriage I knew what I did *not* want. Now, finally, after all these years I know exactly what I do want from my wife:

1. She excitedly wants to have sex, with me and only me, any way, anytime, and anywhere.
2. She *always* takes my side, no matter how stupid I am, against all others.
3. She thinks of me as her hero.
4. She is always happy.
5. She is always happily thinking of ways to make me happy and she is never disappointed because of me.
6. Her life revolves around my schedule.
7. She is grateful to God for the miracle of me being in her life.
8. Her only goal in life is to marry me and be the mother of my children.
9. She greets me each day after work with a kiss and a hug and, "How was your day? Can I make you something to eat before your blow job?"

10. She spreads the word of her undying love and my kind-
    ness and generosity to her family, friends, and the public
    at large.
11. She is always willing to pitch in around the house. No
    job is too menial.
12. She is tightfisted with our money and eternally grateful
    for the gifts I bestow upon her.
13. Her response to my requests is, "Whatever you need,
    honey." And she means it.
14. She would die for me.
15. She loves children.

Things I *Need* from My Wife

I finally, through lots of expensive and painful trial and error, have accepted that in marriage, as in life in general, one doesn't always get what he wants (although on my birthday it would be nice). One has to decide and be happy about getting what he needs:

1. We have sex a couple times a week (occasionally her idea).
2. She supports me when I am absolutely, positively right.
3. She thinks of me as the best man available, at the time.
4. She is not mad, disappointed, or punitive *all* the time.
5. If she's in the mood, she hugs me back when I hug her.
6. She will rub my head 20 percent as much as she does the dogs and lick me 2 percent as much as they do me.
7. She, more often than not, loves me.
8. She can live with the idea of having children with me.
9. When I die, she'll say a couple of kind words at my funeral.
10. She does not go on national television and say that I have a three-inch penis.

11. If something is wrong with the house, she will ask the maids to fix it.
12. She won't spend all our money and complain that I'm working three jobs to make up for it.
13. Although she may threaten to often, she will never leave.
14. She will not kill me.
15. She loves children.

Things 1 Will *Give* to My Wife

I'm a giver, too, so . . .

1. Fifty percent of my money, plus expenses.
2. Seventy-five percent of my soul (sorry it's not 100 percent, but I am in show business).
3. One hundred percent loyalty (yes, it covers that, and that; that, too).
4. One hundred and ten percent of my love (I've given 100 percent before and it just wasn't enough).
5. My life. I would die for her. Seriously. (This is a big one and includes all of my vital organs, which I promise to maintain and care for until needed.)

My Gift

I've learned a little about sports from my costars on *The Best Damn Sports Show Period*, but maybe even more about life ... and death. At the end of March 2002, the same week that John Kruk was happily leaving the show for a month of maternity leave because his wife, Melissa, was having their first child, our buddy D'Marco Farr got some terrible news. His beautiful three-year-old son, Grant, had passed away.

Grant's mom thought he had the flu and called the doctor. He told her to make sure Grant didn't get dehydrated. Didn't sound like a big deal. But when Mom woke up in the morning their little boy was cold. The medical explanation was that he had a serious infection in his intestines that stopped his little body. But basically, D'Marco's only son was running around, playing, laughing, and then he was gone. I had no words for my friend other than the old, "I love you, I'm praying for you and your family. How can I help?" I cannot imagine how it feels. It just doesn't fit in my head. Because it doesn't make any damn sense. It's not the order of the universe. Our parents die, then we die, then long after that our children. It's as if the sun didn't come up one day. It didn't for D'Marco and his wife. I'm sure their sun will come up again, but it'll be a different sun. A little less bright. A little less warm. As I am a man who's always wanted to have children, this scared the hell out of me. Intellectually, I know that horrible events like this are rare, but I just didn't know if my heart could risk taking a chance that someone I loved so incomprehensibly could be snatched from me in the night. How could I possibly survive that? Why would I want to?

Then I realized that I would have to. I'd have to take care of my child's poor grieving mother. I'd have to make her life better. I'd have to make her smile and, eventually, laugh. D'Marco has to survive and actually thrive, because he has a beautiful baby daughter, Trinity. He and his wife were separated, so his tiny little girl is basically saving her 320-pound defensive lineman daddy's life.

At the boy's service D'Marco said something that surprised me. He said that he was grateful. He thanked God for the gift of having Grant in his life even for the short time he did. He talked about the silly things this little boy had done. How he was always smiling. How he loved his family and his toys. We sang his favorite song (something catchy about an elephant) and we all went outside and released a bunch of balloons. Instead of heading for the heavens, most of them got caught in the big maple tree in the front yard. Everybody laughed. I imagined Grant was laughing, too. I realized that D'Marco was right. Every single day with a child is a gift, and instead of being afraid, now I want my gift more than ever.

Regrets

The biggest regrets I have in life are the things I did that hurt other people (how in the hell can anybody, except maybe Frank Sinatra, say that they have no regrets?). I do regret hurting myself here and there, but I feel lucky. I'm lucky for the family I had. I'm lucky for my friends and my career. I'm even lucky that I married the women I did. Because if I'd done things differently, if they'd done things differently, I wouldn't have been in the right place at the right time to meet Shelby, my wife, best friend, soul mate, and the future mother of my children. Where did I go right? Why did I get so lucky? Shelby was right about me, you know; I've got timing, persistence, and a big heart. And sometimes that's all you need. I'm going to be a great dad! Eat your hearts out, Tom Cruise, Tom Hanks, Tom Clancy, Tom Sell . . .